ALASKA RANGE

EXPLORING THE LAST GREAT WILD

Carl Battreall

FOREWORD BY
Art Davidson

MOUNTAINEERS
BOOKS

Mountaineers Books is the publishing division of The Mountaineers, an organization founded in 1906 and dedicated to the exploration, preservation, and enjoyment of outdoor and wilderness areas.

MOUNTAINEERS BOOKS

1001 SW Klickitat Way, Suite 201, Seattle, WA 98134
800.553.4453, www.mountaineersbooks.org

MIX
Paper from responsible sources
FSC® C008047

Printed in China on FSC®-certified paper
Distributed in the United Kingdom by Cordee, www.cordee.co.uk

19 18 17 16   1 2 3 4 5

Copyeditor: Amy Smith Bell
Cover and book design: Jen Grable
Cartographer: Ani Rucki
Front cover photograph: *Evening light paints low clouds and the Neacola Mountains, Lake Clark National Park and Preserve.*
Back cover photograph: *Moose skull and fall colors, Hayes Range*

Front portfolio: page 1, *Wisdom Tooth, Denali National Park and Preserve*; page 2, *Grizzly bear, Denali National Park and Preserve*; page 3, *One of the many tributaries that flows into the Swift River from the west side of the Revelation Mountains;* page 4, *Spectacular ice of the Gillam Glacier with Hess Mountain and Mount Deborah towering above;* page 5, *Shapely Mount Russell, Denali National Park and Preserve*
Frontispiece: *The north face of Mount Moffit reflected in a kettle pond, Hayes Range*

Dedication, facing page: *An unnamed stream cuts through the Nutzotin Mountains, Wrangell–St. Elias National Park and Preserve.*

Back portfolio: page 172, *North ridge of Mount Moffit with Mount Shand on the right;* page 173, *The rarely visited Ramparts, Denali National Park and Preserve;* page 174, *An eroding bank along the Cul-de-Sac Glacier, Kichatna Mountains;* page 175, *Dwarf dogwood, Amphitheater Mountains;* page 176, *Fading light on Silvertip, Delta Mountains*

Library of Congress Cataloging-in-Publication Data
Names: Battreall, Carl, photographer.
Title: Alaska Range : exploring the last great wild / Carl Battreall ;
    foreword by Art Davidson.
Description: Seattle, WA : Mountaineers Books, 2016. | Includes index.
Identifiers: LCCN 2016010351 (print) | LCCN 2016023085 (ebook) | ISBN 9781594859663 (hardcover) | ISBN 9781594859670 (ebook) | ISBN 9781594859670 (Ebook)
Subjects: LCSH: Alaska Range (Alaska)--Pictorial works.
Classification: LCC GB525.5.A4 B37 2016 (print) | LCC GB525.5.A4 (ebook) |
    DDC 917.98/3--dc23
LC record available at https://lccn.loc.gov/2016010351

Mountaineers Books titles may be purchased for corporate, educational, or other promotional sales, and our authors are available for a wide range of events. For information on special discounts or booking an author, contact our customer service at 800-553-4453 or mbooks@mountaineersbooks.org.

ISBN (hardcover): 978-1-59485-966-3
ISBN (ebook): 978-1-59485-967-0

TO MY SON, WALKER

MAY THERE ALWAYS BE WILD PLACES

FOR YOU TO EXPLORE.

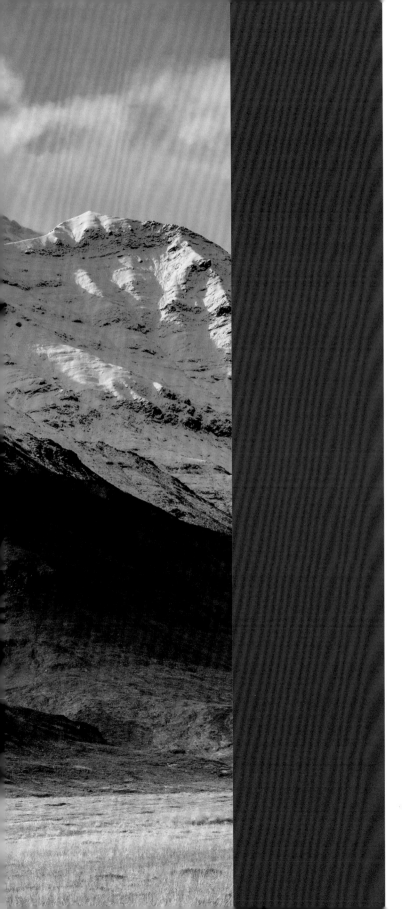

CONTENTS

Map of the Alaska Range 12
Foreword by Art Davidson 15

27 STRING OF JEWELS
Roman Dial

45 THE CONCEPTION OF OUR MOUNTAINS:
THE OROGENESIS OF THE ALASKA RANGE
Jeff Benowitz

Protecting Nowhere 58

69 REFLECTIONS ON FLORA
Verna Pratt

85 WILDLIFE RESIDENTS
Bill Sherwonit

Encounters with Locals 104

113 HISTORICAL SUMMITS
Brian Okonek

Rivers of Water and Ice 130

139 IMPOSSIBLE IS JUST A WORD:
MODERN CLIMBING IN THE ALASKA RANGE
Clint Helander

Flying Low and Slow 156

Acknowledgments 165
Index 166
About the Photographer & the Contributors 168

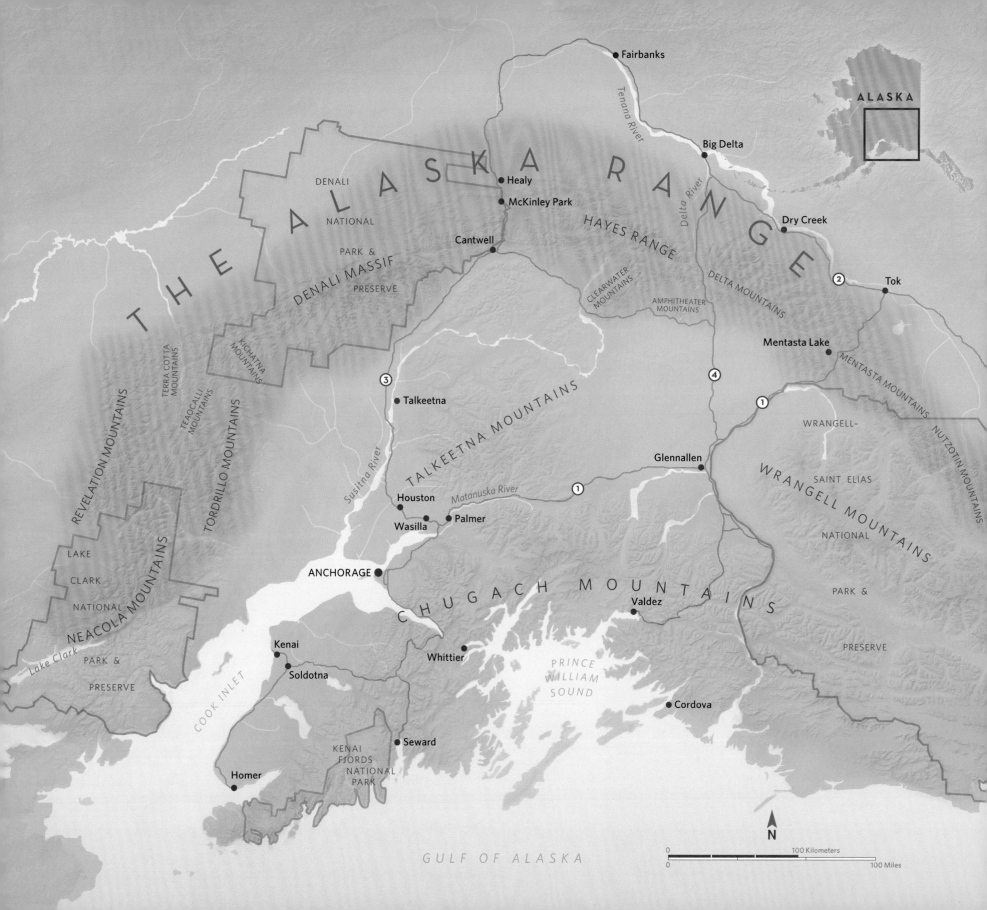

PREVIOUS PAGES Caribou traverse under Peak 10,515, Hayes Range.

LEFT Map of the full Alaska Range

RIGHT The Citadel and Peak 8505, Neacola Mountains, Lake Clark National Park and Preserve

FOREWORD

ART DAVIDSON

In the 1960s the steep granite peaks of the Kichatnas and Revelations at the western end of the Alaska Range called to me and to climbing buddies like David Roberts, Rick Millikan, and Dave Johnston. We were often the first to set foot on a glacier or to climb a peak. What joy we felt as we started up the sheer walls of Kichatna Spire, soaring more than a mile above us.

When I turned to Denali, the massive peak at the center of the Alaska Range, its steeper walls and ridges had been climbed, but no one had tried to climb the mountain in winter. No one knew how cold it would get. Or how hard the wind might blow. Could a person survive, let alone climb through all that darkness, cold, and wind? As we set out in 1967 to make the first winter ascent, it felt as if we were stepping into an unexplored world.

High winds create lenticular clouds and blast the ridgelines above the Black Rapids Glacier during a March ski traverse of the Hayes Range.

15

After four grueling weeks and the death of one of our teammates, three of us managed to reach the summit on the last day of February. We hurried down, but were caught by a storm at Denali Pass. The wind hit us with a deafening roar. It felt as if gravity had shifted and, instead of holding us down, was pulling us across the ice. To get out of the wind, we dug a small cave under the ice.

The storm raged for six days, and with barely anything to eat or drink, our bodies started shutting down. Our friends below couldn't reach us through the storm, and gave us up for dead. When the wind finally ebbed, we managed to stumble down on half-frozen feet.

We had set out to explore a world of ice, cold, and darkness, but it is what we learned about ourselves that has made an enduring difference in our lives. We came away with the deep joy of simply being alive.

YOU DON'T, OF COURSE, NEED to be a climber to be drawn to Denali or to feel the wild pulse of the Alaska Range. We are fortunate that in 1906 Charles Sheldon, a well-educated young man from the East Coast, was wandering the hills near Wonder Lake; he reached the top of a knoll and was overwhelmed by the north face of Denali rising before him.

"The great mountain rose above me, desolate, magnificent, over-powering," he wrote. "There are no words to describe how I felt."

Sheldon was a hunter-naturalist, and as he trekked through the Range, he marveled at the presence of so many wild animals. He also noticed that meat hunters were taking vast quantities of game, feeding half of the meat to their sled dogs and selling the rest to mining camps and in Fairbanks. If this continued, the wildlife would disappear.

LEFT Erosion and freshly exposed glacial ice, Gerstle Glacier, Delta Mountains

RIGHT Huge, towering seracs, Moore Icefall, Delta Mountains

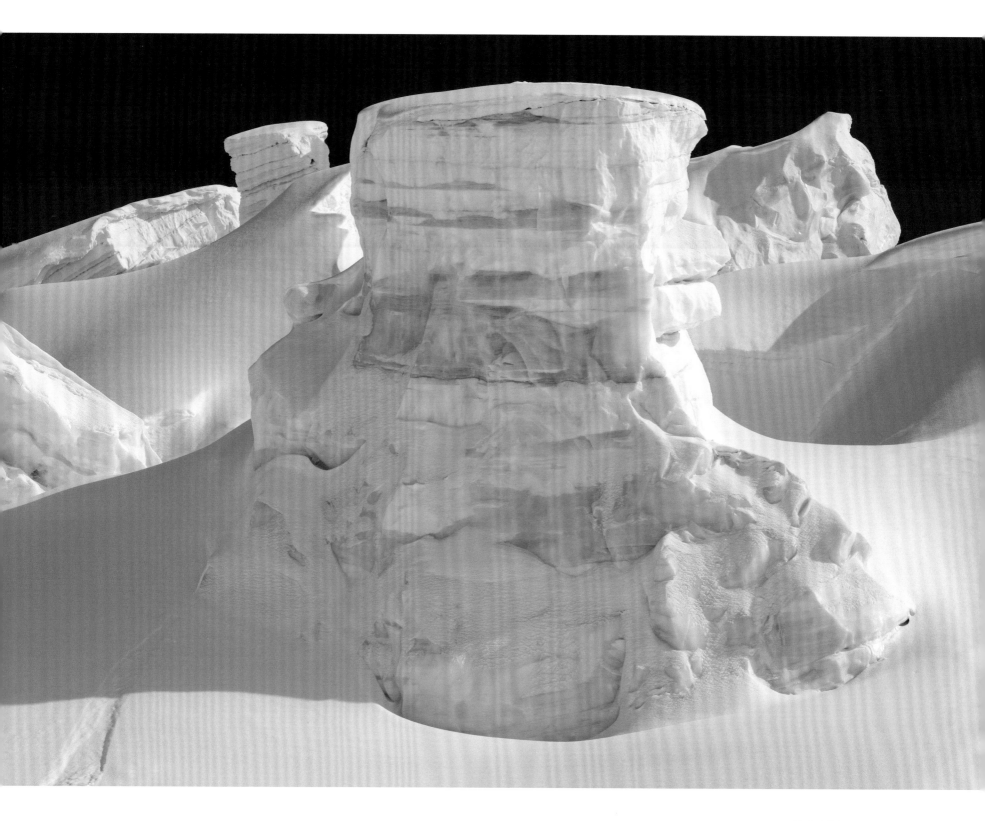

Sheldon had an idea ahead of its time: protect the animals by creating a national park around Denali. He spoke to Congress about "the wild sublimity of the mountains" and "the haunting mystery and isolation of the unknown wilderness."

It took Sheldon ten years to persuade Congress to create Denali National Park. We are indebted to his persistence. We can be thankful, too, for the park managers who followed in his footsteps, and for pioneer conservationists like Adolf, Olaus, and Mardie Murie, as well as Ginny Wood and Celia Hunter, all of whom did everything they could, in their time, to protect the wildness of the Range. However, there is still more to do.

I remember a heartbreaking summer I spent in the park. I arrived in early June, excited to spend the summer filming wolves. But they weren't there! The pack of wolves I'd come to film had been shot over the winter. Within the national park, they were protected, but, being the wild creatures they are, they roamed beyond park boundaries, where killing wolves was legal.

The State of Alaska goes to great lengths to promote tourism, and every visitor hopes to see the iconic wolves of Denali. Yet, the Alaska Board of Game eliminated a no-trapping, no-hunting buffer in 2010. Before the buffer was eliminated, wolves were seen by 44 percent of visitors to the park. Four years later, only 4 percent were able to see a wolf.

Many of the issues concerning the park's wolves and other wildlife stem from only part of it being designated wilderness. In fact, each of the three national parks and preserves either fully or partially within the Alaska Range—Denali, Wrangell–St. Elias, and Lake Clark—have vast untrammeled and ecologically important areas that are not being managed as wilderness. Having wilderness as

their guiding principle would encourage park managers to approach their work with even greater care, alert to any activity, even their own, that might compromise, or even destroy, the very things they try to protect.

Wilderness designation isn't appropriate in every part of Alaska, nor is it a panacea. A wolf can still roam beyond a protective boundary and disappear. Migrating birds die en route to Alaska. The vagaries of climate change affect life everywhere. Still, designating a wild, untrammeled area as wilderness remains the single most effective way to protect the sanctity of a place—and preserve opportunities for visitors to find solitude and a deeper connection with nature.

In the valleys of the Teklanika and Sanctuary rivers, we find the stone tools of nomadic hunters, who viewed what we call wilderness quite differently. These people began finding their way over the Bering Land Bridge when the last ice age retreated about ten thousand years ago. We can see where they camped with their children. We can't reach through the veil of time to hear the words they spoke or the songs they sang. Yet, we know that they lived from the land and were of the land in ways that are hard for our modern minds to fully grasp. They fished for grayling and salmon in the streams, hunted sheep and caribou in the hills, and gathered berries and greens. Like other indigenous peoples, the world around them was imbued with mystery and spirit.

One afternoon, I was hiking in the foothills along the north side of the Range when I came upon a great boulder—an erratic, geologists would call it—that had

broken loose from a distant ridge. It had been carried by an ancient glacier, and came, at last, to rest in a field of grass and clouds. I stopped for a moment and leaned against the rock. I ran my fingers over its face, smoothed long ago by ice and water. As I paused to catch my breath, the stone in all its silence seemed to whisper, "Remember, we are all wanderers here."

FOR YEARS, CARL BATTREALL, WITH cameras in tow, has been wandering the Alaska Range to tell his stories in elusive moments of light that reveal the changing mood of the land or the unexpected presence of wildlife. Imagine setting out to take pictures over a six-hundred mile arc of mountains with a hundred glaciers, thousands of lakes and rivers, wolves and bears, and all kinds of wild creatures—and, in the midst of it all, the highest, and in many ways most fascinating, mountain in North America. Carl's images, along with his notes from the field, reflect the heart and soul of the range, and form the core of this book.

The essays begin with a crazy adventure cooked up by outdoorsman extraordinaire Roman Dial and a couple of his friends—a traverse of the entire range using mountain bikes and packrafts. In "String of Jewels," Roman describes getting into "a rhythm of riding gravel bars and caribou trails westward, pushing up passes, coasting down tundra."

In "The Conception of Our Mountains," geologist Jeff Benowitz reveals his fascination with the wild tectonics that began forming the Alaska Range about one hundred fifty million years ago. He speaks fondly of slab subduction, strike-slip faults, and ancient ocean sediments twenty kilometers deep. "Denali," he writes, "caught a great tectonic wave and has been riding it for six million years."

Wild plant expert Verna Pratt shares her love for the flowers and other plants that first arrived as seeds scattered by wind or water, or were carried here by birds or animals. In "Reflections on Flora," she says, "Just walking among the plants, or having their pleasant aroma fill the air can lift a person's spirits."

In "Wildlife Residents," nature writer Bill Sherwonit revels in encounters with grizzlies, wolves, and other wildlife. "In loose formation, the four wolves headed west across the plains," he writes. "'Out there'—walking ridges and exploring the tundra—is where I too prefer to be."

Brian Okonek and Clint Helander share my love for mountains, and I'd sit around a campfire swapping stories with them any day. Brian and his wife, Diane, have been Denali and backcountry guides for more than twenty years. In "Historic Summits," Brian shares some of their favorite times in the mountains and recounts many of the most historic ascents made in Alaska, while in "Impossible Is Just a Word," Clint, one of the most accomplished climbers of his generation, takes us to some of the most gnarly and scary places in the Range. He speaks of having the courage to follow your heart: "I realized that somewhere upon those distant icy peaks was the path to my self-discovery."

CARL BATTREALL, THESE WRITERS, AND I have been fortunate to be here, wandering about Alaska during a time when we can still see wolves running free, seek adventure in wild places, and find solitude and solace in wilderness. There are still a lot of unnamed mountains out there, a lot of rivers to run. It's a joy to welcome this book that invites us to explore, each in our own way, this range that remains wild and full of mystery—and to help it stay that way.

Tiny grizzly cub in spring, Denali National Park and Preserve

LEFT Ice calved from the Shamrock Glacier, Shamrock Lake, Neacola Mountains

RIGHT Clearing storm on Mount Foraker, Denali National Park and Preserve

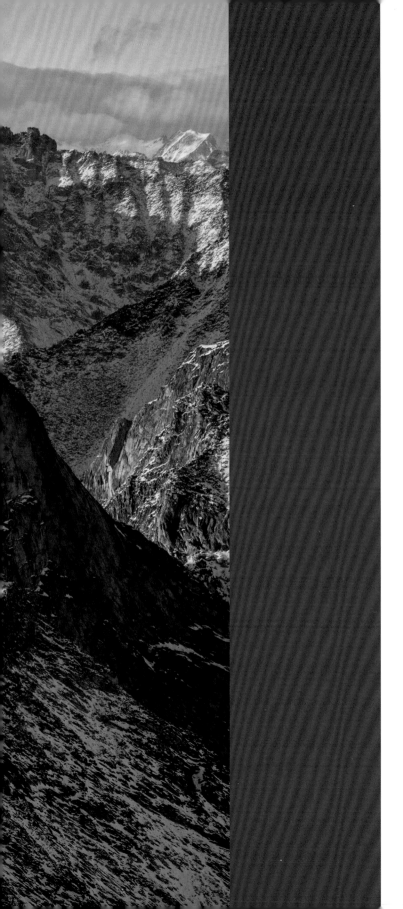

STRING OF JEWELS

ROMAN DIAL

The Alaska Range crowns North America, with its tallest peak, Denali, as it has always been known to the Athabaskans, set among a string of mountain jewels. At 20,310 feet (6191 meters), Denali (formerly known as Mount McKinley) is the centerpiece of a slender spine splitting Alaska in two. Geographically, there are two sides to the Alaska Range, the northern interior and the southern maritime, and historically two ends, Canadian and Russian. The interior side is bone dry (it receives less rain than Phoenix), a desert's worth of precipitation paradoxically supporting crunchy alpine tundra and open forests. The most extremely dry region is the northeast, with low, rounded mountains and few glaciers; the wettest is the southwest, with thick brush and rivers full of salmon. Wide-open vistas of north-side glaciers spill between craggy peaks with Dall sheep, the white, thin-horn, mountain

Among these rarely visited peaks near Merrill Pass, Igitna Peak on the left is in an area known locally as the Hidden Mountains, Lake Clark National Park and Preserve.

LEFT Crevasses and medial moraines on Eldridge Glacier, Denali National Park and Preserve

RIGHT Shadow of Mount Church projected onto the clouds by the morning sun behind an unnamed glacier, Denali National Park and Preserve

denizen, out onto a tundra with grizzlies, caribou, and wolf packs—the wild kingdom visible from Denali National Park tour buses. Creeping up the river valleys are open forests of white spruce and soft willow thickets.

The west and south of the Alaska Range have king salmon and sockeyes, brown bears, alder thickets that resemble the bars of a jail cell, and billowing birch forests with the thorny, head-high shrub known as devil's club. The extreme cold and ground permafrost of the north side force aquifer water to the surface in winter, where it freezes layer upon layer into six- and ten-foot-thick blankets of overflow ice that last into July. Meanwhile, on the south side, the higher precipitation of winter melts off in summer and rushes to the Gulf of Alaska through deep, roaring canyons filled with rivers as big as the Colorado. Instead of dry, alpine tundra,

quaking blanket bogs with floating mats of vegetation can trap unlucky hikers up to their bellies. Moist Pacific air rises, cools, and falls as rain and snow on the south side, leaving it wet, lush, and brushy. The eastern end of the Alaska Range nudges against Canada. Its western end touches Russian-Alaska history.

ON THE FOURTH OF JULY, 1996, Carl Tobin, Paul Adkins, and I set out on mountain bikes to be the first to traverse the six-hundred-mile length of the Alaska Range. We were headed for Lake Clark, a freshwater fjord separating the muscular Alaska Range from the tempestuous Aleutian Range. A bush plane had flown us to a gravel bar five miles from Canada in the craggy Nutzotin Mountains. We bivouacked in meadows wearing head nets to keep mosquitoes at bay.

More than one hundred glaciers disgorge icy rivers from the Alaska Range, blocking overland travel. Without a packraft this range is inaccessible. Carrying a single raft strapped to my titanium bicycle, we were the first to pioneer use of the packraft. At the rivers too deep to ford, we would inflate the raft by mouth. To save weight, we fastened paddle blades to a staff we found at the crossing. I'd ferry my load across first, then return for a passenger, who would help as I brought over the other bicycles, more gear, and the third person. We cooked over fires, ate from a communal pot, drank from our water bottles, and camped under a single tarp without a floor.

In the Nutzotins, tucked in a deep rain shadow behind high coastal ranges, we pedaled for fifty miles historical trails converging on Chisana, a bush community that hosted Alaska's last gold rush in the late 1890s. After packrafting across the Nabesna River, we climbed into the Mentasta Mountains, hiking our bikes between rounded five-thousand-foot summits above a broad plain of spruce forest. We coasted to the brush below on trails worn by Dall sheep. There we pushed along muddy moose trails through willows to a rocky stream bar. At Mentasta Pass, one of three road crossings, we followed mining roads into the Chistochina Mining District. With peaks above 9500 feet (2900 meters) the Delta Mountains, unlike those farther east, feed glaciers fifteen miles long. In the shadows cast by the midnight sun, we crisscrossed glacial rivers below limestone walls (a rock type rare in a range known mostly for granite and schist), headed toward Mount Kimball (10,300 feet, 3140 meters).

A day later on a high ridgeline I took in the vista. To the north, a monotony of mountains poked at the sky.

To the south, a series of tundra plateaus and ridgelines dropped into black spruce forests of the Copper River basin. We climbed over a mountain shown as glacier-covered on our 1950s topo map. Now, a half century later, its slopes and summit were carpeted in green vegetation for the first time since before the last ice age, a sign of climate change. We crossed the Richardson Highway, the original route from Valdez to the Interior, and headed for the Denali Fault, the glacier-filled gut of the Hayes Group. For fifty miles we pedaled, pushed, and sometimes carried along three enormous glaciers. We accelerated on bare ice dusted with loess, a fine sediment offering traction. We followed aquamarine streams cut into the ice or long stripes of broken rocks piled high as medial moraines where side glaciers fed the main flow. A vertical mile above us rose summits of twelve thousand and thirteen thousand feet. The sun shown brightly. Exhilarated, we cruised through the heart of the Alaska Range.

Crossing the spine of the Range, we roped up to safeguard ourselves from crevasse falls, carrying our bikes as we climbed a seven-thousand-foot icy pass. Each of us wore a single crampon for purchase, using pedals and handlebars as crude climbing tools thrust

LEFT Kenibuna Lake, tucked in between the Neacola Mountains and the Hidden Mountains

RIGHT, TOP Cottonwood leaves, Delta Mountains **BOTTOM** Detail of paper birch bark, Mentasta Mountains

into the snow on our descent. High winds and rain motivated us to hustle down and pitch our floorless pyramid among crevasses. Clouds obscured the steep north faces of the sort sought out by alpinists, such as Mount Deborah, Hess Mountain, and 9448 (many of the peaks in this vast range remain unnamed and are therefore known by their elevation figure). Once off the north-side glaciers we established a rhythm of riding gravel bars and caribou trails westward, pushing up passes, coasting down tundra, milking elevation gain until we pushed up the next pass. In the Little Delta and Wood River valleys we saw outfitters' camps, where wealthy hunters from around the world come to pursue trophy sheep, caribou, moose, and bear.

Roughly 350 miles from Canada, we reached Usibelli Coal Mine. Most miners live in Healy, along the Parks Highway and Alaska Railroad. Healy's population swells in summer to serve Denali National Park and Preserve's tourists. The park is six million acres surrounding the Denali Massif, with three million acres of designated wilderness. We followed the Park Road westward for eighty miles to Wonder Lake and Kantishna, where the hilltops provide views of Denali's Wickersham Wall rising eighteen thousand feet (about fifty-five hundred meters) above the tundra plain, the earth's highest rise from mountain base to mountaintop. North of the Denali Massif and beyond Wonder Lake is one of the wildest places in the United States without any dwellings or roads. Protected from hunting for over a century, enormous moose follow veritable animal highways reigned by unnervingly curious grizzlies and wolves.

The south side of the Denali Massif is a vertical wilderness of glacier-carved granite walls, soaring arêtes, and bulky spires—the architectural masterpieces of the

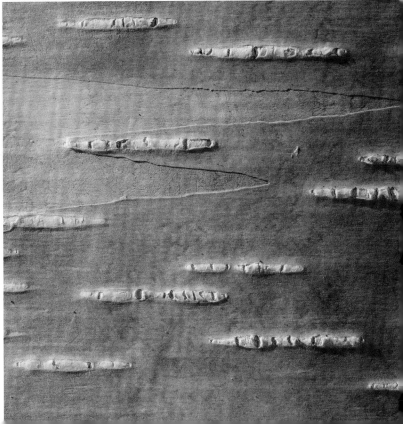

Alaska Range. Principal among these giant gemstones is the mile-deep Great Gorge of the Ruth Glacier, Mounts Foraker (17,400 feet, or 5303 meters) and Hunter (14,573 feet, or 4442 meters), and the lesser satellite peaks along the Kahiltna, Tokositna, and Elderidge glaciers and their tributaries. There, sheer faces, walls, and couloirs define Mounts Dickey, Huntington, and Russell, as well as the Mooses Tooth and Roosters Comb. Denali rises fourteen thousand feet above the six-thousand-foot-elevation flat-belly bottom of the Don Sheldon Amphitheater, a basin fed by five glaciers. These mountains challenge the world's best alpinists and skiers.

Walking the animal trails of the north side, we saw footprints of bear, moose, caribou, and wolves. West of the Denali Massif, near Rainy Pass and the famous Iditarod Trail crossing, the Alaska Range turns southward. Here, a half dozen Yosemite Valleys radiate from a core of eight-thousand-foot peaks in the granitic Kichatna Mountains. Too steep and icy for us, we skirted this scenic highlight to the north, following the Tatina River through the broken, sedimentary Teocalli Mountains. Plains bison introduced in the 1930s have left smooth trails through the forests below the colorful, conglomerate walls of the Terra Cotta Mountains. We cruised along their wild, buffed-out single-track.

South of the Terra Cottas, we bumped along granite bars borne of the Revelation Mountains, a remote group of mostly unclimbed peaks, spires, and glacier-capped walls. The rounded, rocky, golf ball– to basketball-size orbs slowed us as we rode up Sled Pass then descended the Stony River. Paul, his foot injured from weeks of wetness, hopped in the packraft with his bike and some gear. Carl and I pushed onward, wading the chest-deep channels of the Stony. As he passed us, Paul

LEFT Sunset light and rain, taken at 1:00 a.m. in mid-June, Denali National Park and Preserve

RIGHT The sun setting behind Mount Shand, Hayes Range

called out: "I'll see you guys at the lodge!" Three days from Rohn, at Stony River Lodge near Tired Pup Creek, Paul baked us pizza.

Beyond the thirty-mile float down the Stony and somewhere on the Telaquana Trail's tundra, a historical route used by Athabaskans and Russians, we camped. A morning bike problem gave us a late start, but two days later we were along the brushy Kijik River. And soon after that, the finish. Standing on the gravel shore of Lake Clark, I felt mixed emotions: a pang of disappointment now that the traverse was over and we wouldn't be joking and riding and searching the landscape for

passable routes. But, of course, I also felt the satisfaction that comes from achieving a goal. In all, we traveled about eight hundred miles in seven weeks—the length of the Alaska Range from its dry Canadian east to its wet Russian west—the first group ever to do so. We walked in the shadow of its highest peaks, pedaled our bikes through its glacial heart, rafted its angry, gray rapids, and paddled its still, blue lakes. We felt its geography in our bones, tendons, and muscles, moving across the Range's wild landscapes like the animals that call it home. The experience remains in our hearts and souls more than twenty years later.

LEFT, TOP A perfect sundog forms behind a USGS research hut, Gulkana Glacier, Delta Mountains **BOTTOM** High winds on an unnamed peak near Mount Hayes

RIGHT Sy Cloud explores an ice cave formed inside a crevasse, Ruth Amphitheater, Denali National Park and Preserve.

Mount Johnson, Ruth Gorge,
Denali National Park
and Preserve

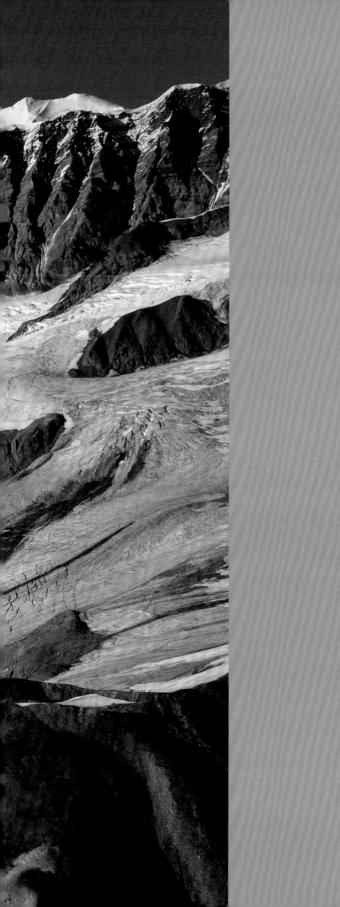

THE CONCEPTION OF OUR MOUNTAINS

THE OROGENESIS OF THE ALASKA RANGE

JEFF BENOWITZ

Clouds, lingerie for the mountains. This first line of a poem I wrote may be a justification for my indiscretions, or simply an acknowledgment of the flaws of the human condition. Everyone has a vice. A passion that borders on obsession, one that leads to risky behavior, that makes plunging into a fast-moving glacier-fed creek—your rational fears drowned out by the sound of crushing boulders—a happy place. For the past twenty-five years, I have sacrificed one pair of boots a year, acquired a pile of broken ski poles and skis along with a few

The surge-type Susitna Glacier descends from the south flanks of Mount Hayes, the highest mountain in the Alaska Range outside Denali National Park and Preserve.

frostbite–blackened misshapen toes, and gained a tangle of surgical metal clink—all in pursuit of time with my mistress. Rain so hard it stings like mosquitoes, mosquitoes so thick they sound like rain on a sun-damaged tent fly. Finding myself trapped up high in the Alaska Range by the weather and by my desire. Ah, the joy of rolling over on the tundra awakening to a valley floor rainbow.

My relationship with my first love, the Alaska Range, has bloomed like roadside fireweed. Having spent the winters of my youth chasing summits and crafting routes from the Nutzotin Mountains along the Canadian border to the Kichatnas of the western Alaska Range, I passed many a summer thunderstorm day at the University of Alaska–Fairbanks library studying maps for hidden faces, untrodden climbing gems. Over the years, despite my climbing partner's disdain, I started pausing on ascents to simply touch the mountains. Soon my pack became filled with rocks, the rainsticks of our natural world, recording narratives of ocean's collapsing, continents colliding, mountains rising, falling to only rise again. More and more my mountain romance has morphed into getting to know the Alaska Range through revealing the stories held by the mountains' cold stones. The geological history of orogenesis (the birth and life of a mountain range) entices me to continually seek a relationship with the landscape I call home even as my cartilage disintegrates to sand.

The high peaks of the Alaska Range and its sister structure, the strike-slip Denali Fault, create an approximately seven-hundred-kilometer arc (more than four hundred miles) across Interior Alaska. The broadly east-west trending, topographically segmented range can be divided into the eastern, central, and western Alaska

LEFT A silt-rich stream and a clear-water stream converge near the Gulkana Glacier, Delta Mountains.

RIGHT Strange light above Mount Foraker, Denali National Park and Preserve

Ranges by regions of high and low topography. The majority of the topography in the eastern range lies north of the seismically active Denali Fault, which slices through the earth's rigid outer shell, known as the lithosphere. Broad Pass separates the eastern from the central range, where the majority of high topography lies south of the Denali Fault. To the west, there is a bend in the Denali Fault with Denali and Mount Foraker on the inside. Southwest of the bend, the north-south trending western Alaska Range takes an abrupt ninety-degree turn away from the Denali Fault.

This asymmetrical physiography has attracted the attention of geologists for more than a hundred years. Many of the well-known peaks are named after these early geologic explorers who spent their lives studying the history of the Alaska Range by foot, horse, canoe, and ski. All modern geologic papers and maps on the formation of this range are built on the efforts, bushwhacking traverses, glacier creek crossing, and rock sampling of Fred Moffit, Alfred Brooks, and their contemporaries. Like modern climbers, they divided the Alaska Range into two during the first half of the twentieth century. Moffit spent about forty years mapping

the eastern part, while Brooks fished for rocks along the slopes of Denali, working their way through the past. Geologic time is like waiting for a bush plane to come get you after six weeks in the Range—stretched slow: their findings started to unfold the full story of the growth of the Alaska Range, which began about 150 million years ago.

ANYONE FAMILIAR WITH THE BLACK shale and slate of the Muldrow moraine, or the crumbly rock capping the Ruth Gorge and the granite domes of the Revelations, will be glad to know the preferred geological term for this rock formation is the Black Crap. During the late Jurassic (about 150 million years ago) there was a subduction zone near the present-day Alaska Range and no southern Alaska as we know it. South of today's Alaska Range, there was a large oceanic basin where mostly mud was deposited for approximately forty million years. Eventually continental sands and gravels were added to the mix. Technically these basin sediments are referred to as the Kahiltna Assemblage to the west and the Nutzotin Basin to the east, but the Black Crap is a more fitting name.

Riding on the back of the Paleo-Pacific Plate, thousands of kilometers south of Alaska, was a "fast" approaching super terrain (a region of crust with a unique geological origin) made up of oceanic volcanic islands, today referred to as Wrangellia. For a biological perspective on how far southern Alaska has traveled to get where it is today, while hiking in Wrangellia (in the Wrangell Mountains, for instance), keep your eyes out for tropical coral fossils. As Wrangellia approached paleo-Alaska, the subduction machine simultaneously shut off along the present-day Alaska Range and jumped to the south near its current location. The shut-off subduction became a region where two land masses are stitched (or sutured) together; geologists refer to this broad area along the Denali Fault system as the Alaska Range suture zone. As Wrangellia slammed into Alaska, the sediments of the Kahiltna and Nutzotin basins were piled high as the terrain wreck drove northward. If climbing these mountain piles of Black Crap seems daunting (Mount Brooks and Mount Moffit are classic examples), keep in mind that today these ancient oceanic sediments are over twenty kilometers thick in some places below the surface.

The continued stitching of southern Alaska (Wrangellia composite terrain) with interior-northern Alaska happened over the next forty-five million or so years. Today the suture zone is an area of weak crustal material, the slightly metamorphosed sandstone and mudstone of the Kahiltna Assemblage, the Nutzotins, and a paleo-subduction zone. The lower Cantwell formation (eighty-five to sixty-five million years old) in Denali National Park is a terrestrial basin that records the final throes of this collision. Dinosaurs actually roamed this depression as mountains rose and were eroded

under the shadows of large, erupting volcanoes. This long-lived volcanic arc spanned much of Alaska and is responsible for many of the granitic plutons that make up the crests of the Alaska Range. Though the Cantwell Basin was located at nearly the same latitude, the climate was quite different (warmer and wetter) during late Cretaceous Alaska from today.

Southern Alaska never fully sutured to Interior Alaska, with a crustal scale fault still separating Anchorage and Fairbanks (mirroring the cities' different political ideologies). Known as the Denali Fault system, it has been active since at least sixty-five million years ago as primarily a strike-slip fault. These types of faults are predominately responsible for translating blocks of crust (bodies of land delineated by faults) horizontally, resulting in minimum mountain building. Yet large mountains (reaching elevations greater than six thousand meters) exist along the Denali Fault, so what gives? The next great indentor to bang on Alaska's southern subduction door was an active, spreading oceanic ridge that arrived around sixty million years ago. Oceanic ridges sit on top of oceanic plates as subaqueous mountain ranges; these bathymetric highs don't go down subduction trenches without a fight. Their subduction results in crustal collision and flattening of the slab (low-angle subduction of the down-going plate). Variations on the flat slab subduction theme have pretty much ruled the Alaska tectonic roost throughout the Cenozoic.

The flat slab of the Resurrection–Kula Plate Ridge did leave its mark on southern Alaska, but the real party maker was the thermal effect of the spreading ridge itself. A fair deal of the domal western Alaska Range was created as a result of this effect, technically called a slab window. When an active spreading ridge subducts,

A boulder balances on the edge of the Gillam Glacier, Hayes Range.

there is a gap in the down-going slab where super-hot asthenosphere (fluid mantle) upwells lead to increased volcanic activity and large-scale topographic doming. The Tordrillo and Kichatna mountains are related to this early Cenozoic tectonic event. Throughout the western Alaska Range there are also mafic dike swarms (streaks of black lines across a field of granite) related to the accompanying slab window event. After this ridge subduction event there was a period of plate reorganization and flat slab subduction of warm, young oceanic crust. The thirty-five-million-year-old (give or take) volcanoes north of Broad Pass are remnants of this tectonic period. We think little was happening in terms of mountain building during this time, but we might be mistaken. Based on limited evidence, around forty million years ago there may have been a fair deal of strike-slip movement, magmatism (volcanoes and pluton formation), and possibly orogenesis taking place. If you are looking to leave your mark on the geologic history of the Alaska Range, collecting samples from the granite of Mount Foraker (which dates to this era) might provide some answers.

THE ALASKA RANGE WE KNOW and love truly began to rise about twenty-five million years ago. The last major foreign land to crash into the southern Alaska subduction machine was the Yakutat microplate, comprised of overthickened oceanic crust. Because of this unusual thickness (about eleven to thirty kilometers thick, compared to the standard seven kilometers for oceanic crust), the Yakutat microplate is buoyant oceanic plateau crust and hence has subducted at a shallow flat angle. This resulted in the presence of arc volcanoes along the northern edge of the Alaska Range suture

zone about five hundred kilometers inboard from the active subduction trench. The Jumbo Dome in Healy (estimated to be one million years old) is one of these volcanoes.

The initiation of the flat slab subduction of the Yakutat microplate had a dynamic effect across Alaska from the trench to the Brooks Range. The Alaska Range volcanic arc shut off at this time as the Wrangell volcanic arc started up in earnest, creating some of the largest volcanoes the world knows today. From the southern coastal ranges to the Tordrillo Mountains to Denali to Mount Deborah over to the Nutzotins and even in the northeastern Brooks Range, the crust bucked in response to the arrival of the Yakutat indentor, which led to a dramatic period of rock uplift. The Denali Fault itself experienced a change in character from a sleepy strike-slip structure to a relatively fast superhighway (progressing about ten millimeters a year), moving crustal blocks with the fault being the double yellow lines.

Strike-slip faults do not normally lead to the production of large mountain ranges, because by definition these geological structures are primarily responsible for the horizontal transport of crustal material. However, when there are crustal blocks in "fixed" relative positions or kinks along a strike-slip system, a significant component of horizontal motion can be taken up by vertical slip along the main strand of a fault and splay faults (subsidiary faults that connect to the master fault at depth). The high peak region of the eastern Alaska Range (the Hayes Range) is one of these relatively fixed crustal blocks. Mounts Deborah, Balchen, and Hayes are sandwiched between the Hines Creek Fault and the main strand of the Denali Fault. At this position

LEFT Granite patterns in the Kichatna Mountains, which at more than forty million years is some of the oldest topography in the Alaska Range, Denali National Park and Preserve

RIGHT Polychrome Hills composed of volcanic rocks formed between fifty-five and sixty million years ago, Denali National Park and Preserve

the mountains will not be translated out, leading to persistent deep rock uplift as the Denali Fault is pushed to the north by that pesky Yakutat microplate. In fact, if you are climbing in the Hayes Range along the north side of the Denali Fault, you may be grabbing hold of highly deformed mylonite rocks (look for garnets and quilted rock fabrics) that were at a depth of about fifteen kilometers fewer than twenty million or so years ago. Just imagine what the mountains would be like were it not for erosion.

Denali is the albino moose of the Alaska Range, taller by three thousand feet and broader than all the other peaks in the Range. Many geologic factors contribute to how Denali got to be so big and so strikingly different from the surrounding mountains. The combined forces of the Yakutat microplate and a change in the vector of the incoming Pacific Plate six million years ago are the far-afield drivers for the most recent episode of rapid uplift in the central Alaska Range. Plate tectonics aside, the main contributing factor to Denali's astonishing bulk is more local: a kink called a restraining bend in the Denali Fault. As the fault moves at an average rate of four to eight millimeters (about a quarter inch) per year, the mountain is essentially "stuck" inside this bend because the vertex of the bend is also moving west (at a slightly slower rate of about three

millimeters a year). Hence Mount Foraker (17,400 feet, 5303 meters) is essentially a paleo-Denali. Additional factors also play a role in Denali and Foraker's high elevations but have substantially less influence. Denali's crustal block has essentially caught a great tectonic wave and has been riding it for six million years.

The Revelation Mountains and neighboring sub-ranges are also being driven skyward because of their fixed position relative to the Denali Fault system. The crust south of the fault, referred to in geological circles as the Southern Alaska Block, is rotating counterclockwise along the right lateral Denali Fault. To the west of the Revelations, the Bering Plate is rotating clockwise. The intersection of these two rotating crustal bodies is a classic space problem. With nowhere to go but up, we get the majestic Revelations.

AS THE WORLD PLUMMETED INTO an icehouse environment around three million years ago, glaciers spread across the Alaska Range. The thick deposits of eolian loess of Interior Alaska started to accumulate as the glaciers began to grind down the mountains. Because of the erosive power of glaciers and the accompanying isostatic response (crustal rebound), glaciers crafted the Alaska Range we see today. The carving of deep valleys, like the Ruth Gorge, has led to a decrease in the average elevation of the Range (which is now about 4260 feet, or about 1300 meters). Yet when six kilometers of crustal material is removed, the isostatic response (because of the lowering of the crustal load) results in only about one kilometer lowering of average elevation (remove six kilometers and five kilometers "bounce" back up). Because the removal of crust is generally focused in valleys, glaciers can lead to

higher peaks even as the landscape is getting broadly subdued.

The majority of the glaciers along the Denali Fault are surge-type glaciers, meaning that they generally move even slower than normal glacial-pace glaciers, but occasionally they surge forward at rapid rates (such as meters a day). One of the distinguishing features of surge-type glaciers are loop moraines. The Susitna Glacier is a classic example. Why glaciers surge, and why surge-type glaciers are often associated with fault systems, is an open-ended question worth pursuing.

NOVEMBER 2, 2002. AS I CRAFTED my way up a granite wall in Yosemite National Park, my cabin back in Fairbanks was all a-shake. The magnitude 7.9 Denali Fault earthquake was one of the largest strike-slip fault earthquakes ever recorded. In addition to rupturing about three hundred kilometers (about one hundred ninety miles) of glaciated terrain from Mount Nenana to the Nutzotins, the earthquake resulted in huge rock landslides along the Black Rapids, McGinnis, and Gakona glaciers.

My fondness and desire to fondle the Alaska Range has grown as we geologists become closer to unraveling the when and how of the Range's topographic development. Like running the last few meters to crest a summit along a ridge to capture the view on the other side, and then running on toward the next hump for the same, scientists bathe daily in this bright light of the unknown. The draw of the Alaska Range is that distant red granite buttress draped with snowscape and the fossilized rock turned over twice as we seek our personal view across the horizon and into the past: the Alaska Range suture zone might not be stitched, but we are bound to this landscape we call home.

Glacial erratic near the Gakona Glacier, Delta Mountains

PHOTOGRAPHING THE ALASKA RANGE
PROTECTING NOWHERE
CARL BATTREALL

Wedged in between the volcanic Tordrillo Mountains and the granite towers of the Revelations is an area unofficially known as the Hidden Mountains. The name was given to this isolated pocket of peaks and glaciers by the early explorers of the Tordrillos. For the past decade I have obsessed over visiting this place so isolated and remote that it had few names. I could find fewer than five known recorded expeditions, and even fewer published photographs. The Hidden Mountains were true wilderness, an alpine paradise.

Year after year I postponed trying to reach them; other regions of the Alaska Range felt more "important" and certainly more accessible. But as my final season of Alaska Range project expeditions arrived, I made plans for an extended stay in the mountains of my dreams. Reaching the Hidden Mountains is only possible by plane, and a very expensive trip at that. Landing options are limited, as are skilled pilots willing to fly there. There are lakes and gravel bars, but they are all on the perimeter, nothing in the Interior, in the heart of the mountains. I scoured maps and Google Earth.

There were a few glaciers that would allow a ski plane, but I wanted to go in the summer, and by mid-June the low-altitude glaciers would be bare and unsuitable for a ski landing. And then I stumbled upon a satellite image of a Caribbean-blue lake tucked in a narrow valley. It looked promising: long enough and with enough depth. The lake didn't have a name, nor did any of the glaciers or surrounding areas. It was perfect.

Two weeks before our departure, one of my partners broke his leg. It took a while for him to fully commit to not going; he too had become obsessed with the idea of exploring, essentially, nowhere. His wife (a third partner in this scheme) decided it was best she stay home too. I scrambled to find more participants, an impossible task on such short notice. Most of my regular partners didn't have a thousand bucks lying around for a trip to nowhere. The cost to charter the plane was $3200. Split in thirds, the fee was reasonable, but by myself I couldn't do it.

For a few days I was devastated. This unchartered territory was one of the only areas in the Alaska Range I hadn't tried to visit. There were many lifetimes' worth of trips to be pursued. I had resigned myself to the fact that I would only scratch the surface of the Alaska Range, but I really wanted to explore the Hidden Mountains.

What makes them so irresistible is that they are just that: hidden. Hidden from those who no longer have curiosity. Hidden from those who need knowledge, guidebooks, and photographs to justify going someplace. Hidden from those only chasing names, records, altitude. The Hidden Mountains, and the majority of the Alaska Range for that matter, represents something that is missing from most people's wilderness experience: *real* wilderness. Almost the entire Alaska Range is trailless, roadless. Isolated wilderness is something to be celebrated, something that needs to be preserved.

MY PARTNER, SY, AND I decided to visit the Nutzotin Mountains on the far east end of the Alaska Range, tucked behind the monstrous Wrangell Mountains, right on the Canadian border. The area was well traveled during Alaska's gold rush days, but for the past fifty years or so, the majority of the Nutzotins have seen few, if any, visitors. We decided to visit a clump of unnamed peaks and glaciers. We had grown tired of the relentless deluge of information that was constantly being fed to us through every form of media. There isn't any originality in modern living anymore, no discovery. The answer to almost any question is only one click away. With our smartphones now almost an extension of our bodies, it is impossible to get lost—rescue is nearly always at our fingertips. We wanted a free experience in the mountains, no preconceived routes decided by others.

On our next expedition, we decided we would only bring our outdated map and a compass—no GPS, no SAT phone, no beta, no information. We brought gear to climb

and explore but had no set goals; we simply wanted to wander in the mountains. We wanted to connect with ourselves—a seemingly impossible task in the modern world. I even considered leaving my camera behind, but upon reconsideration I decided photography was my job and we were going to the Alaska Range!

For a week Sy and I climbed unnamed mountains, explored valleys, and followed clear creeks to their source. We went wherever our curiosity led us, our sense of wonder our guide. After a few days we quit looking at the map. We used our skills to choose routes, drank water with our hands, laid our heads anywhere we pleased. We got wet, cold, scared, and tired. We laughed hard and smiled big.

We had countless encounters with wildlife, both big and small, including watching a red grizzly dig up roots with its powerful claws, an apprehensive porcupine delicately crossing a stream, and a fox hunting for ground squirrels, tracking their squeaks across the tundra. Clouds and shadows danced along the summits of distant peaks in the evenings, while Dall sheep crossed precariously on the loose slopes below, with grace and confidence we could only wish to possess in the mountains.

What we were doing was pure living. Wandering, guided by curiosity, was essential to our health. We weren't outsiders, we weren't spectators watching from the road, trail, or on the couch. We were actually existing *in* nature. We learned things that no website could ever teach us. Lessons about ourselves and about coexisting on Earth. We, humans, are just one of the many creatures that walk the earth—not better, not unique, only different. Some researchers believe that many children are missing a key experience in their childhood development: unstructured time in nature. Terms like "nature deficit disorder" have been coined to define a growing epidemic.

But the epidemic is also prevalent in adults. In fact, maybe more so. Adults need unstructured time in nature too—time in raw, unspoiled wilderness. Some people have become ambivalent toward wilderness. They want it to exist but are satisfied with landscape wall calendars and an occasional nature documentary. Nature photography, writing, and filmmaking is supposed to inspire people to get out and experience nature.

Fear-mongering enforces the destructive idea that wild places must be tamed, cultivated, and populated. Some people are simply afraid of the wilderness, which is ironic because it is no more dangerous than many modern cities. Amazing, modern outdoor gear is available that can handle any weather nature can throw at you; ultralight tents, stoves, and clothing make traveling in the backcountry easy and quite luxurious. Science has proven that wildlife should not be feared—respected, yes, but not feared.

In Denali National Park and Preserve, the paved paths and buses are crowded with people in search of that "amazing experience" they were told Denali and Alaska offers. Every summer day, hundreds of people ride on the buses in search of wildlife, in search of an occurrence that might change them, enlighten them. Very few get off the bus and yet by walking twenty minutes away from the road, in any direction, they could find that life-altering experience. They could connect with the wilderness,

touch the soggy tundra and see its abundance of life, hear the silence, and feel the cold breeze. They could watch nature's clock, the sun and clouds, drift slowly across the deep blue sky.

Off the path is where we learn, the place we have soul-developing adventures. After you experience the backcountry only a few times, it will become a necessity in your life. Satisfy your desire for wild places by spending more time in the mountains, desert, and forest. The Alaska Range has many such pockets, much of it unprotected state and federal land. This land is open to the highest bidder for resource extraction, particularly coal and gold. It seems nearly impossible that Americans will be able to convince the government that we desperately need these lands protected. Some factions are still attacking the lands that received federal protection thirty years ago.

The Alaska tourism industry is constantly growing and has shown itself to be a viable, economical alternative to the short-term dwindling of natural resources that many factions continue to pursue. The fact is, we the people need to change. The few citizens who are standing and uniting are busy trying to protect the land we already have. Who is going to fight for Alaska's last, unprotected wild places? I wish I had an answer.

As the human population explodes past seven billion, we have reached a tipping point. The modern world is simply unsustainable. While science has created innovative ways to help people, many of us are finding that our technology-driven world is unfulfilling, shallow. The modern world survives on the backs of the poor, fueled by cruelty to animals and the destruction of nature. We are slowly realizing that maybe living disconnected from the natural world is not the healthiest nor the happiest choice.

Technologies exist that allow us to coexist with nature without destroying it, to live happily without causing suffering to others. Why do we continue full speed ahead on a dead-end course? When we spend time in the wilderness, we learn about ourselves. Humans are amazing creatures, but we are flawed. We possess attributes not found in the other residents of our planet. Greed continues to drive us toward our demise, and it exists only in humans. If we could just replace our want, our desires, our greed, with what we *need,* the whole world would change.

On my final aerial photography flight, at last I headed to the Hidden Mountains. We flew over painted hills of orange and gray. Above shrinking glaciers and the lake that I had long hoped to visit, the blue waters were more beautiful than I could have imagined. We also flew over a large camp, an exploration camp in search of the next big mine, an alternative to the notorious Pebble Mine, a major threat to Bristol Bay, the largest salmon fishery on Earth. But this mine was in the remote wilderness, away from watchful eyes, away from those dammed hippies, tree huggers, conservationists, fishermen, guides, Alaskan Natives, poets, and photographers.

It was a naïve dream: There are no hidden mountains.

Meltwater stream on the surface of the Gakona Glacier, Delta Mountains

LEFT A fin of exposed ice, Black Rapids Glacier, Hayes Range

RIGHT Meltwater on the Backside Glacier, Denali National Park and Preserve

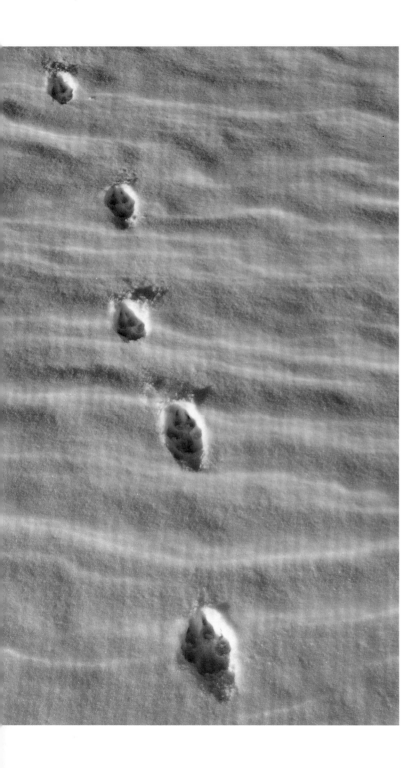

LEFT Fox tracks, Nutzotin Mountains, Wrangell–St. Elias National Park and Preserve

RIGHT The monstrous Mount Hesperus towers over the Revelation Mountains.

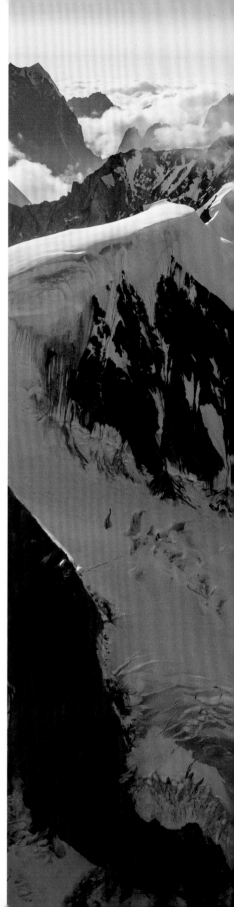

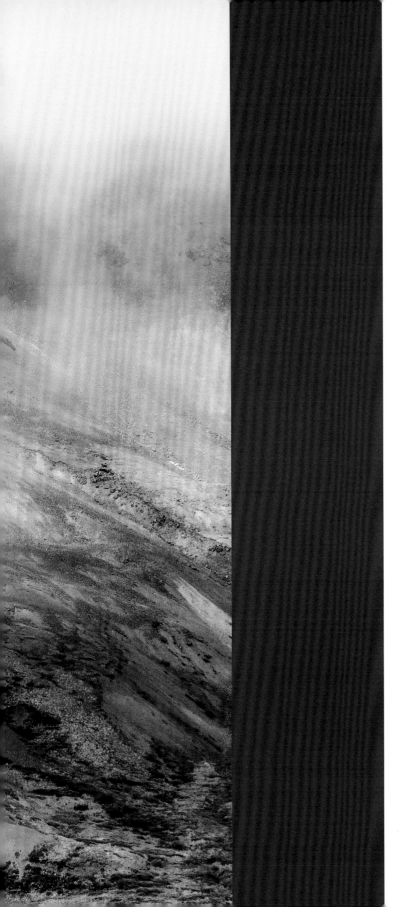

REFLECTIONS ON FLORA

VERNA PRATT

Alaska is noted for its variety of scenic vistas from the rain forests of Southeast to the rocky cliffs of the Aleutian Islands in the west and on north to the Arctic Ocean. There isn't a place across the state that doesn't have great beauty, but there is nothing more awe-inspiring than Alaska's many mountain ranges. Like a giant magnet, they draw you toward them. It doesn't matter how many snow-covered peaks you have seen or how many times you have been to the same valley; there is always the intrigue of seeing something new. Every range is different and has its own character and charm, but the allure of the Alaska Range captivates me over and over again.

Sun, rain, and mist add to the polychromatic landscape near Highway Pass, Denali National Park and Preserve.

From the magic of its magnificent peaks that have been scoured and shaped by glaciers through millions of years, to its tiny streams that trickle down the mountains to join larger streams that meet raging rivers on their way to the sea, these mighty mountains are filled with breathtaking beauty. Pebbles and stones collect to form ripples and pools as water meanders through vegetation and boulders. All kinds of fascinating life-forms—from large animals down to the very smallest plants and insects—coexist beautifully here. Some are remnants of past generations. Each life-form attracts people eager to explore all aspects.

Like Carl, I am a photographer, intrigued with the vastness of this area and how the lighting, created by a change in weather, alters a familiar scene. Rapidly changing conditions surprise many hikers who start out on a sunny, pleasant day. Nature paints a beautiful palette, and these mountains provide a wide variety of rock formations with stunning colors. An artist's paradise to be sure.

However, I am most drawn to the plants that make these rugged mountains their home. Plants choose the area where they live, usually based on where the correct amount of moisture necessary for survival is. But some plants rely on certain minerals present in the soil for survival, and these are often produced by the rocks. An amateur plant aficionado can predict what plants could be in an area by the color of the rocks. Light gray or tan rock slopes usually signify the presence of lime. Very fussy plants might not grow anywhere else except where these minerals exist. Seedlings will not survive if conditions are not right, and existing plants can weaken when the soil has been altered.

EACH HABITAT IN THE ALASKA RANGE has its own collection of plants that like the conditions produced by that specific environment. Some of the plants were left by glaciers; the rushing glacial streams change course at will, which forces plants into a new location, often with totally different growing conditions. Some of the plants were seeds scattered by wind or water, and others were carried by birds or animals.

Bogs, meadows, low-elevation woodlands, and the alpine zone exist throughout the Alaska Range, with unique and thriving flora within each habitat. Bogs usually are created by underground ice or water that doesn't drain well; they are very cold, slowing down the decaying process. For composting to occur, you need four things: plant material, heat, water, and air circulation. Wet, soggy, cold soil prolongs the process of composting. Bog plants, such as bog rosemary (*Andromeda polifolia*) and bog cranberry (*Vaccinium oxycoccos* var. *microcarpus*), prefer to have water at their feet, and the acidity of the immature soil is often needed to produce blooms. They will grow differently if moisture is not provided and might die if they are not capable of adapting to the change. Meadows maintain an abundance of moisture from deep snow cover that lingers late into spring. This produces large leafy plants—such as alpine forget-me-not (*Myosotis alpestris* ssp. *asiatica*), frigid shooting star (*Dodecatheon austrofrigidum*), and Alaska boykinia (*Boykinia richardsonii*)—that decay more rapidly and build deep soil.

Low-elevation woodlands with their ample foliage on plants and deciduous trees are home to many plant species, including dwarf dogwood (*Cornus canadensis*), large-flowered pyrola (*Pyrola grandiflora*), and twinflower (*Linnaea borealis*). This habitat has all the ingredients to

produce good composted soil and microorganisms that many plants rely on for healthy plant growth. Some plants are totally reliant on mycorrhiza, which is a fungus that attaches itself to the roots of plants. This helps the plants to better absorb minerals and water and protects the roots from other fungi. This is a symbiotic relationship, as the plants in return provide carbohydrates for the fungus. Spotted lady's slipper (*Cypripedium guttatum*) and yellow paintbrush (*Castillejas caudata*) are perfect examples.

My favorite part of the Alaska Range is the fascinating above–tree line alpine zone. Here tree line usually occurs at about twenty-five hundred feet and has many different growing conditions—the most obvious being wet and dry tundra, which includes treeless areas that are sometimes flat but very well drained and have low vegetation. Along alpine ridges and rocky outcrops most of the plants are low, small, and isolated from each other by rock clusters. Many of them are very small and could easily be overlooked when not in bloom. Their tiny clusters of leaves are camouflaged to look like rocks, which successfully protects them from predators. The best example of this is ciliate saxifrage (*Saxifraga eschscholtzii*), which is difficult to see even in bloom. I have adopted the common name of barnacle saxifrage for this plant, however, because of the diminutive tight clusters of leaves.

The petite anadyr draba (*Draba stenopetala*) grows on gravelly scree slopes and has minute clusters of leaves that look like a small jagged rock. By growing close to the ground, these small wonders of nature avoid harsh winds and absorb additional heat from the rocky soil. Shifting soil is common in gravelly areas, partly from spring snowmelt and from animal activity. Many of the

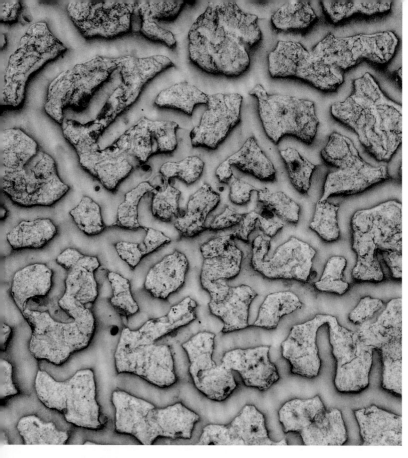

plants that grow here help to hold the slopes together by growing in large mats. Here is where mountain-avens (*Dryas octopetala*) and alpine bearberry (*Arctostaphylos alpina*) spread their roots in the loose soil; both are circumpolar plants (that is, they are species that can be seen around the world at the same latitude). The vivid red fall bearberry foliage signals summer's end.

Many of the plants that grow in the eastern part of the Alaska Range are also found in the Rocky Mountains as far south as Colorado but at a much higher elevation (at ten thousand to fourteen thousand feet). Only those that can adjust to warmer and dryer conditions will survive there, as most alpine plants prefer cooler weather even in summer. Their seeds may need stratification, which is a long cold period that prompts them to germinate when it becomes warm again. Because much of the soil in the mountains is very young in maturity, it does not contain much compost, and the plants in this zone of the Alaska Range grow slowly. When the sun is out, the very shallow rocky soil heats up, allowing the small amount of plant material to decay, enrich the soil, and retain moisture. This varies from spot to spot, depending on the amount of decaying matter, the type of rocks available, and the direction of the sun. Plants on a mountain's cool, damp, and more acidic north side, where composting takes more time, are very different from those growing on the sunnier south side. Small evergreen shrubs such as bell heather (*Cassiope tetragona*) and crowberry (*Empetrum nigrum*) favor the north-side environment. Plants that prefer more mineral-based soil, especially lime, usually prefer the south side and lime-encrusted rocks.

The Alaska Range is a melting pot of plants from around the world. The extreme western end of the

Alaska Range contains some plants that occur in the mountains in the Aleutians and Japan, such as weasel snout (*Lagotis glauca*) and Arctic primrose (*Primula exima*). These are plants of wet tundra, which often has standing or slow running water moving through it as the permafrost beneath it does not allow it to drain. The middle section of the Range has a collection of plants seen in northeastern Asia as well as in Alaska's North Slope, such as mountain forget-me-not (*Eritrichium nanum*) and northern larkspur (*Delphinium brachycentrum*). Many of the plants

that exist in the alpine zone are circumpolar. Visitors from Norway or Iceland will find the familiar subshrub Lapland diapensia (*Diapensia lapponica*) on many Alaska mountaintops.

Other plant species have limited distribution in the world, and the Alaska Range has a few endemics in the alpine zone, such as polar milk vetch (*Astragalus polaris*), Alaska douglasia (*Douglasia alaskana*), and denseleaf draba (*Draba densifolia*). Some of the more significant and slightly more widespread species that are endemic to the Alaska Range and the Yukon Territory include

northern kittentails (*Synthyris borealis*), Gorman's douglasia (*Douglasia gormani*), and Nootka milk vetch (*Astragalus nutsotinensis*).

THE LEANER SOIL, HIGH IN the alpine zone of the Alaska Range, has few nutrients and composted soil, so it produces much smaller plants. Summers get progressively shorter, and summertime is when you notice the plants more and appreciate their efforts to endure and reproduce. Many small, isolated populations of unique plants, such as northern candytuft (*Smelowskia borealis*) and nodding campion (*Melandrium macrospermum*), are here; there is always some concern for their survival if a sudden climate change occurs. Often it is human activity that damages plants in sensitive areas. These can be restored by growing replacement plants, replanting, and closing the area to foot traffic, but we cannot control the results of an overall change in climate. As the days get warmer, as has been happening over the past fifty years, trees and shrubs in the Alaska Range are now surviving at higher elevations, but it could take most plants centuries to make the necessary changes to adapt.

Plants would need to develop longer, more absorbent root systems and succulent leaves. Most of them currently have tough, weather-resistant roots, stems, and leaves or tiny hairs to keep them warm and to trap moisture. While the animals and birds that rely on these plants for food might slowly migrate to a more suitable location, the plants themselves cannot do that. The tiny alpines would likely succumb because they already have so many special adaptations for survival in the opposite conditions. To survive as they are, given climate change, they would need to move up the mountain. Some would become extinct from desiccation and predation. It is sad to think that sometime in the future these small treasures may be lost forever, and there is little we can do to prevent it. This would be an enormous loss to the alpine zone in the Alaska Range. Many people would never know that these plant species had ever existed. Only a small percentage of people oversee plant survival in Alaska's wilderness areas, yet plants have always played an important part in human existence.

Dozens of wild plants, such as Eskimo potato (*Hedysarum alpinum*) and Parry's wallflower (*Parrya nudicaulis*), found in the Alaska Range were traditionally used for food by villagers and settlers and are relatives of cultivated plants we eat today. Roots provided needed starch; vitamin-rich leaves and a tasty variety of berries packed powerful punches of nutrients. Many of these wild plants are still used today, especially in Native villages, and berries from the Alaska Range are eagerly harvested by people all over Alaska.

Recent plant survival efforts have emphasized caution on overharvesting, so harvesting roots of plants is discouraged among the public. Most people now buy their produce in stores rather than spending hours foraging for food in the Alaska Range. However, anyone harvesting wild plants, for any purpose, should practice good ethics, so the species can continue to exist. A good rule to follow is an old American Indian tradition: one for the bird, one for the bear, and one for me. Eventually those that went to the bird and bear would go to the seed.

Other plant species native to the Alaska Range, such as common wormwood (*Artemisia tilesii*) and Labrador tea (*Ledum palustre*), were found to be useful medicinally and cosmetically. At one time all medicines were derived from plants, but the use of plants in medicine is limited today. The strength of the chemicals in plants can be variable, depending on the soil in which they grow; this can make some species dangerous to use. Fatal errors taught early users that they needed safe medicines and consistent dosage.

FROM THE FOOTHILLS TO THE tall peaks, the Alaska Range has a vast array of plant species. There are countless ways to appreciate this extensive flora. Just walking among the plants or having their pleasant aroma fill the air can lift a person's spirits. From the first sprig of spring grass to the last falling leaf, a bright tapestry of color spreads over the Alaska Range. It doesn't matter what the season or weather; there is something special awaiting you out there.

Moraine patterns, Yentna Glacier, Denali National Park and Preserve

LEFT Fresh snow near the Trident Glacier, Hayes Range

RIGHT Wet moose calf, Denali National Park and Preserve

LEFT Waterfall Creek, Clearwater Mountains

RIGHT Denali reflected in a pond, Petersville Road

WILDLIFE RESIDENTS

BILL SHERWONIT

Driving my mud-splattered car through Sable Pass, a place of tundra foothills known to be frequented by grizzly bears, I noticed two shuttle buses stopped along the gravel road, their signal lights flashing golden in the gloomy autumn afternoon. I slowed and pulled to the shoulder. The drivers and their passengers were looking at wildlife. *Maybe they've spotted some bears,* I thought, scanning for anything that resembled a grizzly. The fortunate owner that fall of a rare road permit, I was homeward bound after three nights on the north side of the Alaska Range, in the heart of Denali National Park and Preserve. Already I had spotted most of the larger, grander wildlife you can hope to see on the Range's northern flanks: caribou with their antlers

A beautiful bull caribou is surrounded by fall colors in early September near the Hayes Glacier, Hayes Range.

shedding velvet; Dall sheep white against the browns, reds, and yellows of volcanic hills; a giant-antlered bull moose feeding on willow; and, best of all for this bear lover, a blond, berry-fattened grizzly hungrily stripping blueberry bushes of their dark fruits beside the Park Road, then casually ambling onto the gravel less than fifteen feet from my front fender.

After turning off the engine, I followed the gaze of the bus drivers and their passengers to the right. Unable to locate anything that looked like an animal, I walked over to the nearest driver, who held up three fingers. I mistakenly took this to mean a family of three bears: a mom and her twin cubs. "Wolves," he said, shaking his head. "But they just went over the ridge. Six in all." I simply couldn't leave, knowing six wolves were passing through the area. I waited five minutes, maybe ten. Then I decided to play a hunch. Back in the car, I did a U-turn and retraced my path through Sable Pass, looking for an angle that might better reveal the wolves as they moved across the hills. Finally I pulled over, leaving plenty of room for traffic to pass. Putting binoculars to eyes, I scanned the ridge. For a minute or two I saw nothing but rock and tundra and clouds. Then, to my delight, a dark, four-legged form appeared, silhouetted against the sky. A lone wolf trotted along the ridgetop. I could make out little detail, except that the wolf's body was dark gray. For no reason, I decided the animal must be a male. He descended the hill and angled toward a dirty remnant snowfield that filled a north-facing gully. The wolf stopped frequently and repeatedly dropped his head as if smelling the tundra, then glanced around, in no hurry.

Another shuttle bus arrived. I told the driver about the wolf and described his position. The snow patch

helped the driver locate the animal, so another busload of people got to share in the treat. By now the wolf had returned to the ridgeline. He briefly paced back and forth, then dropped out of sight. I had watched the wolf for ten minutes or so, at a distance where he was barely visible with the naked eye. Yet this "encounter" would remain firmly fixed in my memory. Years into the future, I would likely recall it as the highlight of this trip into Denali. Something about seeing the wolf on that far ridge seemed especially exciting. My hunch had played out, but it was more than that. I preferred to see the wolf atop that far ridgeline instead of ambling down the middle of the road, trailed by buses and cars. Though the park's narrow road corridor presents the best opportunity to see Alaska's wolves, the Alaska Range's wild backcountry is the animal's home, where he is closest to his essence. Seeing the wolf in remote, wild terrain stirred my imagination. It was almost as if I'd been carried out there, far from the road and its busloads of tourists.

"Out there"—walking ridges and exploring the tundra—is where I too prefer to be when in Denali and other parts of the Alaska Range. Away from the crowds, immersed in wildness, sensing a lupine joy.

A SURPRISING VARIETY OF MAMMALS, birds, and fish—and also the region's lone amphibian, the wood frog—inhabit the broad sweep of the Alaska Range, from its most humble foothills to the mountain chain's great heights. The occasional grizzly bear or moose is sometimes observed on the snow- and ice-covered slopes of Denali, and mountaineers recount stories of ravens and other songbirds that have landed on the High One's snowfields (the smaller birds have inevitably been

thrown off course by severe storms while migrating through). Though adventurers may encounter wildlife almost anywhere in the Alaska Range, the best place to do so is on its northern side, where Denali National Park's single road crosses open-tundra expanses. The most intensively studied portion of the Range, Denali is inhabited by at least 39 species of mammals, and more than 160 varieties of birds have been observed here, though some are considered "occasional" or "accidental" visitors.

For every grizzly, wolf, Dall sheep, golden eagle, or peregrine falcon that enthralls us, dozens of other smaller or more secretive animals are key members of the Alaska Range's varied ecosystems, essential to their healthy functioning. One of those small and seldom-seen residents is the collared pika, named in part for the light gray "collar" of hair that rings this mammal's neck and shoulders, contrasting sharply with the much darker brownish gray head and back. With its small, stocky body, short legs, and rounded ears, the pika resembles a large mouse or a guinea pig, but it has no tail and is most closely related to rabbits and hares. The English name, pika, is apparently derived from a Russian term that means "to squeak." That makes good sense, because the pika is known for its loud, squeaky call.

Because they are secretive and uncommon creatures even where their populations are healthy, pikas usually reveal their presence to us humans by their high-pitched "bark," issued as a warning when a perceived threat appears. Considered gregarious animals, pikas live in loose colonies, though individuals tend to stay within their own half-acre territory except during the spring-summer mating season, when neighbors of

the opposite gender are welcomed. I've never observed more than a single pika in any area and then only briefly. They're most often seen perched on the rubbly piles of rocks that are their homes, whether talus debris on steep mountain slopes or boulder piles along alpine streams. Once a friend and I even discovered a pika along the rocky margins of the Denali Park Road, visible to us walkers but hidden from the thousands of people who drove past its home each day.

Though curious from a distance, pikas dive for cover when approached. But if patient, you can watch a pika cautiously reemerge and clip, then nibble the stems and leaves of grasses and wildflowers, or collect and carry plant clippings into underground storage caches, to build stacks of food that researchers say may reach two feet high and two feet across. Because pikas are not hibernators, such "haymaking" behavior takes over their lives in mid- to late summer. At the peak of their harvesting, they may make a trip every minute or so from den to feeding area and back. Rarely do they travel more than ten feet from their protective rock piles, ever wary of predators—primarily weasels and raptors—and never too sure about humans, either.

IT CAN BE ARGUED THAT Dall sheep are the perfect symbol of what famed biologist Adolph Murie called the parkland's "wilderness spirit." These snow-white mountain sheep are iconic images of the Alaska Range's wild assembly of animals. Dall sheep are what drew naturalist-hunter-conservationist Charles Sheldon to the Denali region in 1906. Their preservation, as much as anything, inspired him to seek park status for this wildlife-rich part of the Range, a quest that led to the creation of Alaska's first national park—then named

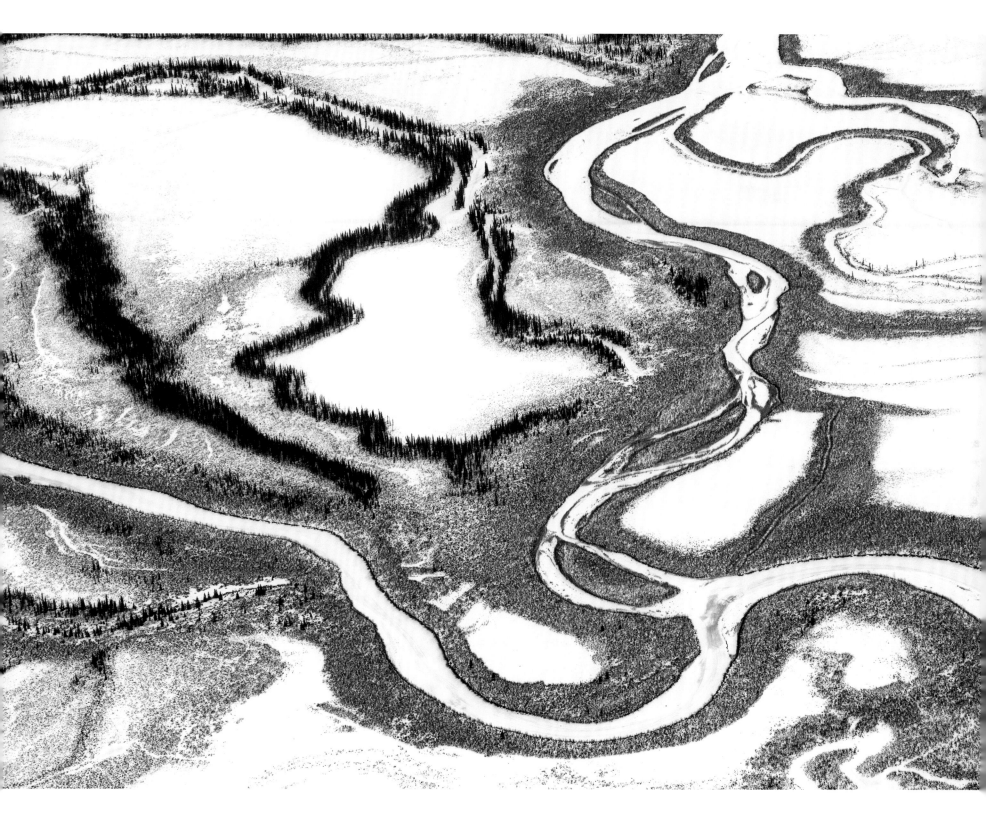

Mount McKinley—in 1917. Later in the park's history, severe Dall sheep declines in the 1930s and 1940s caused great alarm and forced park officials to confront wildlife-management policies that favored one species (sheep) over another (wolves). Thanks largely to Murie, the sheep crisis—and the species' eventual recovery—ultimately led to a strengthening of ecosystem rather than favored-game management in Denali; here, all native species would be protected. Nowadays, around two thousand Dall sheep (give or take a few hundred) inhabit the park's alpine heights. The majority live on the park's northern side, in both the Alaska and Outer ranges. Because the Park Road borders some of their prime habitat, these sheep provide visitors an excellent chance of seeing the region's "wilderness spirit."

A small percentage of Denali's Dall sheep actually cross the Park Road on seasonal journeys between the park's two mountain ranges. These migratory sheep

spend their winters in the Outer Range, where snow-fall is light and high winds keep exposed ridges free of snow. In May or June they form groups of up to sixty or seventy and cross wide lowlands to reach the Alaska Range's northern foothills for summer's green-up. There the sheep remain until late August or September, when they retrace their steps. Adult male and female members of the species live apart except during the early winter mating season, which occurs in November and December. Just prior to the rut (and occasionally throughout the year), mature rams butt heads in fierce battles that scientists say determine their place in the band's social order and, consequently, its breeding order. Adult females, too, will sometimes knock heads, apparently to determine social rankings. Ewes produce a single lamb in late May or early June. As the birth approaches, a pregnant ewe heads for steep, rugged terrain, where predators are less likely to be.

Both sexes of adult sheep have horns, though only males grow the large, sweeping, and outward-curling horns. As rams mature, their horns form a circle when viewed from the side and reach a full circle or "curl" in seven to eight years. The amber-colored horns are male status symbols, and large mature rams can be seen displaying their horns to other sheep. Females' horns are much shorter, slender spikes. Unlike the antlers of moose and caribou, horns are never shed; they continue to grow throughout a sheep's life. Growth occurs only from spring through fall; winters are marked by a narrow ridge or ring. The age of sheep can therefore be determined by counting the annual rings (also called annuli). Though rams may live into their mid-teens and ewes their late teens, biologists consider twelve to be very old for a wild sheep. Dall sheep are grazing animals that feed on a variety of plants, including grasses, sedges, willows, and other herbaceous plants; in winter they survive on lichens, moss, and dried or frozen grass. They prefer to stay up high, in places that combine open alpine ridges and meadows with steep slopes, because their hill-climbing skills make it easier to escape predators in such sheer, rugged, mountainous terrain.

HERE'S A FACT THAT WOULD likely shock many folks: more people have died crossing streams in Denali (four) than have been killed by grizzlies (one). That speaks to the species' wariness—and tolerance—of people. Still, the great bear demands our attention and respect, and rightly so. This is a creature that blends enormous strength and an apex predator's killing tools—teeth and claws built both for tundra digging and tearing flesh—with surprising agility and speed. The grizzly's explosive bounds and agile quickness even when chasing ground

Moose in a kettle pond near
Canyon Creek, Denali Highway

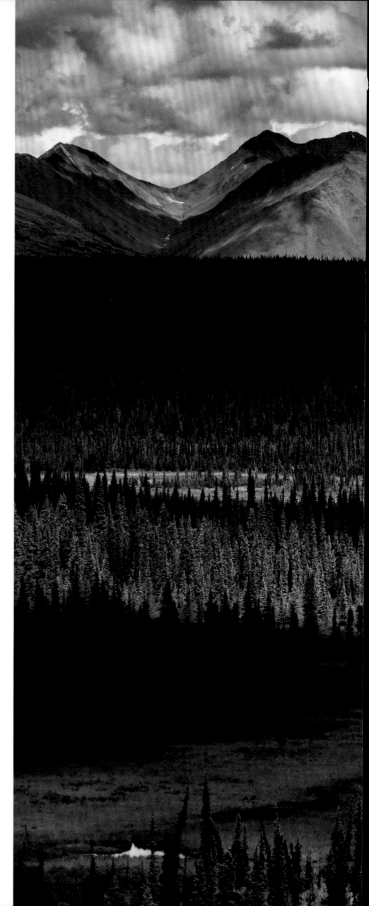

squirrels make clear the futility of a person trying to outrun a bear and the reason that park rules prohibit visitors from approaching within three hundred yards of a grizzly when on foot or bike. Really, there's no need to do so: the bears are easily seen from the Denali Park Road.

It seems a paradox that animals needing such large swaths of wilderness hunt ground squirrels, dig for roots, graze on berries, nap, and sometimes even chase caribou or interact with wolves all within easy view of the Park Road and its large, noisy buses. But much of the road passes through prime grizzly habitat, making it easier to spot wildlife—especially large, blond to dark

chocolate animals weighing up to six hundred pounds. Many of Denali's grizzlies have grown habituated to people and bus traffic. Humans and their vehicles are neither a threat nor a source of food. Busloads of people come and go, and the bears go about their business— mainly that of gathering food. Grizzlies, it has been said, are "eating machines." This is especially true in the subarctic region that includes the Alaska Range, where they must survive an entire year on the food they eat during their five- to seven-month waking period. An adult male bear that weighs 450 pounds when leaving its den in spring is likely to weigh 550 to 600 pounds when it reenters a den in October. The diet varies with the season: roots, emerging plants, winter-killed animals, and moose and caribou calves are favorite foods from spring through early summer; from mid-July into fall and early winter, the number one choice is berries, especially blueberries and soapberries. As den-up approaches, a grizzly may consume hundreds of thousands of berries daily, eating almost nonstop for up to twelve hours a day. Only rarely do grizzlies prey on adult moose, caribou, and Dall sheep, and the ones they do kill are often older, sick, or injured animals.

THOUGH THE ALASKA RANGE is best known for its large mammals, it is also home to a massive, cosmopolitan community of birds. Nearly 170 species have been identified in the park, though only two dozen or so live there year-round. The great majority spend their winters in warmer climes and come north to Alaska for the breeding and rearing season, largely because of an abundance of food: Alaska's summertime explosion of insects and the animals that feed upon them (small fish, small rodents, and shrews). Birds migrate here from numerous parts of the world: Asia, Central and South America, Hawaii, even Antarctica. The world's greatest long-distance flier, the Arctic tern, may travel up to twenty-four thousand miles in its annual seasonal pilgrimages between Antarctica and Alaska.

People visiting the Denali region or neighboring parts of the Alaska Range in the fall are likely to witness one of the north's most spectacular migrations: the passage of lesser sandhill cranes through these mountains on their return south to wintering grounds in the American Southwest, Texas, and Mexico. Among the most iconic of Alaska's animals—and the only one of the world's fifteen crane species to inhabit this part of

the world—lesser sandhill cranes stand three to four feet high, with wingspans of six to seven feet. Besides their great size, sandhills are known for their dance moves; among the most unusual and captivating of avian displays, crane dances have been celebrated and in some instances copied by cultures around the world and across time. Also famous for their loud, distinctive voices, which have a haunting, primeval quality, sandhill cranes have a rattling, bugled, or trumpetlike sound, though to my mind their voices have a guttural "roaring" nature and that is the word I've settled upon. These calls are usually what bring cranes to our attention; like most birds, they're heard before they're seen. Because they've evolved a long and looping windpipe that amplifies their voices, sandhills can be heard from long distances, sometimes miles away.

The first time cranes grabbed my attention, more than a quarter century ago, great flocks of them passed over the Alaska Range while I hiked in Denali. Their loud roaring calls pulled my awareness from the ground into the distant heavens, while stirring thoughts of more ancient times. Years later, I spent two days in the cranes' captivating company while camped at Wonder Lake, where a friend and I gazed upon—and listened to—tens of thousands of sandhill cranes as they flew past 20,310-foot (6191-meter) Denali and other snow- and ice-covered Alaska Range peaks. We couldn't have asked for a more dramatic setting, and the cranes' performance topped our highest expectations. They traveled in long skeins and Vs that seemed to change shape as birds shifted positions, sometimes forming large, curving arcs before resettling into the more classic angular Vs. Occasionally a flock would break formation and begin to rise in great swirling, roarking columns while

lifted on thermals, both disorienting and beautiful to watch. We first heard the soft calls of distant cranes—more of a soft purring than harsh roarking—shortly after noon and for the next two hours there wasn't a moment when cranes weren't visible or audible somewhere in the sky. For the next day and a half they came in waves, sometimes in small family units of three or four, other times in flocks of two hundred to three hundred, maybe more.

ANOTHER AUTUMN SPECTACLE IN THE northern foothills of the Alaska Range is the annual moose rut, an especially fascinating time to observe the largest member of North America's deer family. Like clockwork, it begins in late August, when bulls begin to lose the velvet from their antlers. This is also when they dig "rutting pits"—shallow, elongated depressions into which they urinate. Both bulls and cows may wallow in such pits or splash the urine-mud mixture onto their antlers, head, neck, and shoulders. Around September 1, dominant bulls stop feeding and begin their search for cows. At midmonth, they become more vocal and start to actively herd cows into breeding groups. Their grunts—described by biologists as "croaks"—are made while traveling alone, during courtship, or in response to rival bulls. Breeding normally begins the last week of September and reaches a peak about October 1. The rut gradually winds down and ends by October 10.

The breeding groups of cows are sometimes called harems, but they are more of a loose aggregation: "The bulls don't really have control over the cows," says longtime moose researcher Vic Van Ballenberghe. "A cow can leave a bull if she's serious about it." The largest aggregation he has seen numbered thirty-four moose:

RIGHT Ice flows in the Chulitna River while the aurora dances above Denali, Denali State Park.

twenty-two cows and twelve bulls. Besides the dominant bull, other males—called "satellite bulls"—hang out along the margins and sometimes breed with cows on the periphery. It's nearly impossible for a bull to stay in charge of an aggregation throughout the rut. During the peak, the dominant bull may be challenged several times during the day—and the fighting eventually takes a toll. "It's sort of like being in a bar," Van Ballenberghe observes. "Sooner or later, somebody's going to come along who's tougher." Confrontations begin with displays and threats and eventually escalate into sparring and, sometimes, fierce fights. Injuries are part of the ritual. About one-third of the dominant bulls are harmed, some fatally. Few bulls live beyond age ten or eleven, while the average life span of cows is fifteen to sixteen years; some live to be twenty or older. When the rut has ended, the moose split up. Younger bulls remain with the cows, while the more dominant bulls go off in loose groups of up to ten animals.

The rut is one of two periods when moose are most dangerous. The other is during the calving season, late May to early June. Cow moose are fiercely protective of their newborns and dangerous enough that Denali Park staff issue "moose warnings" to visitors. The rule is different than for bears: if a moose appears aggressive, run away from it as fast as you can, to get out of the animal's personal space. Weighing thirty to thirty-five pounds and cinnamon-colored at birth, moose calves grow quickly and weigh three hundred to four hundred pounds by the fall, with darker brown coats like those of adults. By maturity, a large bull may weigh one thousand to fifteen hundred pounds, stand seven feet high at the shoulders, and carry antlers sixty to seventy inches across and weighing seventy pounds. The

antlerless cows are only slightly smaller, seven hundred to eleven hundred pounds.

ON A BRIGHT AND WARM September day, I sat with four other people on a tundra knoll and with binoculars scanned a broad lowland expanse named the Plains of Murie. Wolves had been reported in the area, including some pups, and we were hopeful of a sighting. The Grant Creek Pack, among Denali's best-known wolf families, inhabits this area, and for many years during the early twenty-first century its members were frequently sighted; howling was sometimes heard along the Park Road. But in 2012, one of the pack's breeding females was trapped just outside the park and a second breeding-age female died of old age. The death of those two wolves led to a social breakdown, and several of the remaining wolves dispersed.

Though the family unit ultimately survived this trauma and a new breeding female eventually joined the group, the pack's behaviors and habits changed in substantial ways and its members haven't been nearly as visible since then. This disruption coincided with a steep decline in Denali's overall wolf population, followed by greatly diminished wolf sightings along the Park Road. Wolf advocates point to hunting and trapping on state lands just outside Denali National Park as a significant factor and have sought additional protections for park wolves. Meanwhile, state wildlife managers and biologists say that from a population perspective, there's "no biological problem" either inside the park or within the broader Alaska Range and dropping wolf numbers in Denali are more likely tied to declining numbers of prey. Whatever the cause, Denali's estimated wolf population in 2015 was the smallest since annual surveys were begun in the mid-1980s. Visitor sightings are the lowest they've been since the 1990s—a substantial change at a park widely recognized as the best place in Alaska for people to see wolves in the wild.

Our own group of wolf seekers got lucky that autumn day in 2014: first we spotted a lone wolf loping across the tundra below us, its body a mix of pale gray and white. As we continued to watch, a smaller, darker gray wolf—what biologists would likely call a subadult—joined the first. And then, to our great delight, two pups appeared out of some willow clumps. The three younger wolves had been hiding, waiting at a rendezvous site for the older wolf to return from a hunt. In loose formation, the wolves headed west across the plains below us. We watched them for nearly a half hour, before they disappeared among dense willow thickets. We kept watch another hour, maybe longer, before resuming our own explorations, our day brightened and spirits lifted by the presence of wolves.

Outwash plain from the Polychrome Glacier, Denali National Park and Preserve

Sy Cloud improvises, heating water over an open fire, after our stove broke during a winter trip in Denali State Park.

ENCOUNTERS WITH LOCALS
CARL BATTREALL

It was pouring rain and we were in need of a flat spot to make camp. I looked off the ridgeline and spotted a perfect perch near a rambling creek. A large bull caribou lounged in the tundra. As we got closer, he refused to acknowledge us. Setting up our tent and unpacking our gear did not seem to upset him.

For the next two days we shared a small piece of wilderness with the beautiful bull. We may have been the first humans this caribou had ever seen. He was such a powerful creature, a perfect specimen—polished gray fur over sculpted muscles, with towering, symmetrical antlers. He appeared brave and fearless, irresistible to females, respected by other males. Healthy and fat, rolls rippled down the bull's neck, but he was clueless to our power. I felt guilty occupying his space; he had established a rutting hole and was intent on staying there, waiting for females or another rival male to come sniffing up.

His natural characteristics made him an obvious target for hunters. I wanted to chase him, torment him, let him know that humans were not kind, that we were predators. I wanted him to be scared of me. I wanted him to run. But I also wanted to photograph him, to coexist with him in the wilderness, to simply survive and exist in remote wilderness together. After two days of sharing this space, we continued on our journey.

As we departed, I looked for a sign, an acknowledgment from the animal that said, "Yeah, you're cool." Of course, I got nothing, not even a parting glance. And that was exactly how it should be. Caribou are curious creatures. In the rolling tundra, they are not quick to run when encountering humans. A large group will often split up, with a few caribou coming close to investigate the strange bipeds, while the others run around in a panic, waiting for a signal from the investigators. Eventually they will distance themselves but stay in view, keeping track of the humans' whereabouts.

My first encounter with a caribou was in a most unusual place. We were at the toe of a nameless glacier in the Delta Mountains, putting on our crampons, when the cool glacier breeze delivered a foul smell. We assumed it must be a carcass, but as we began our ascent up the gentle glacier, we noticed small piles of what looked similar to dark mounds of melting chocolate: scat, the source

of the stench. The glacier was covered in it. As we crested a small rise, we saw sixty caribou lounging on the ice. It took a few moments for them to notice us, as we were downwind. Once we were spotted, however, they rose and without much fanfare casually meandered away to the other side of the glacier.

Caribou spend much of the summer on the glaciers and snowfields of the Alaska Range, because there they can retreat from the heat and unforgiving bugs of the mountains. Glaciers also provide a great vantage point—there is nowhere for predators to hide. For me, caribou sightings have become a good omen; they are essential representatives of this wild place. When I am in their habitat and don't encounter them, I feel like there is something wrong, something missing. Stumbling upon some scat, tracks, or an antler shed—just knowing they exist in the landscape I am passing through—is enough to bring a smile to my face.

THE OTHER RESIDENT OF THE Alaska Range that has made a significant impression on me as a wilderness traveler and a photographer are the bears, the main wildlife attraction for visitors to Alaska. Most Alaska Range brown bears are grizzly bears, meaning they reside in the Interior, away from the food-rich coast and its salmon-choked streams. They live a tough life, as food is scarce and difficult to obtain. Grizzlies can be very protective of even the most meager of food sources. They are more unpredictable than the coastal bears and less tolerant of people.

I rarely photograph grizzly bears when traveling in the backcountry. In fact, I prefer never to see one. Encountering a bear changes the trip dynamic. You can't help wondering where it is and whether it will show up uninvited to dinner. Most of my photographs of grizzly bears have been taken from the Park Road in Denali National Park and Preserve.

This is really the only way to safely photograph Interior bears up close. These bears simply ignore the buses and cars, although their behavior changes when they spot or smell people outside of the buses. I have seen it many times—they get a whiff of a person and suddenly they become alert, on the defensive, keeping tabs on the human's whereabouts, unable to focus on their previous task (usually looking for and consuming as much food as possible).

So far, my encounters with grizzly bears have been civil, pleasurable. I can't say the same for my meetings with black bears, however. Like caribou, black bears are curious creatures. One July my father and I visited Shamrock Lake on the edge of the Neacola Mountains. This remote location has seen few visitors. We landed on the shores of Kenibuna Lake, adjacent to Shamrock Lake but larger and not packed with ice like Shamrock. We set up camp along the lake, underneath the large terminal moraine of Shamrock Glacier. On the second day we saw three bears on top of the moraine. One bear was chasing the other two. It was a sow trying to chase off her older cubs. It was time for them to go on their own. We would see these bears often.

My dad was a firefighter, with years of experience flying in helicopters. He is also a firearms expert, having shot guns for years. A lifetime of helicopters and guns means that he doesn't hear too well anymore. We were hanging out at camp when the bears showed up on the ridge. My Dad had his back to them, when suddenly they came crashing our way. I could see the willows shaking as they approached.

"Dad, the bears are coming!" I yelled. No response. I called out again, but he did not understand. He heard my third exclamation, but it was too late—one of the bears had arrived. The black bear and my father did a little dance around a lone willow before Dad made his way to me. We stood together for a few seconds then slowly walked backward toward our tent, talking firmly to the bear. It appeared the young bear was totally baffled by us and all of our stuff. He showed no aggression or apprehension, just utter curiosity, but he was getting a little too close, so we chased him off with loud words and flying rocks. Unfortunately, we became the most interesting thing in the area and the bear continued to visit us. He never bothered our food stash or cook area; he focused on our tent and the area where we hung out.

I finally pepper sprayed the bear, and we thought that would be the last time we would see him. But that night we were lounging on the lakeshore, photographing Arctic terns, when I heard the unnatural sound of collapsing metal. It took a few seconds to recognize the noise: it was the distinct sound of a tent peg. "Dad, the bear is at the tent!" I yelled and we dashed over to our camp. The tent was collapsed, completely flat except for a large moving mound in the middle. I yelled "bear!" and the mound froze. Claws punctured the tent, tearing a hole big enough for the bear to stick his head through. He looked at us with the most dumbfounded look.

Pistol aimed and ready, Dad said, "I don't want to shoot this bear." "Don't," I said, "just scare him." My dad shot right next to the bear, to no response. I resorted to throwing large rocks and pelted the bear right between the eyes. That worked, and he bolted into the willows. We were never sure if this bear was the one we had chased off before or its sibling. Either way, it left a trail of wreckage in its wake. The tent was destroyed. Our sleeping pads were sliced into claw-width strips, sleeping bags in shreds. Our only option was to call the pilot and have him come get us early.

So many of the world's great mountain ranges are losing (or have already lost) their wild residents. My close encounters with wildlife have been one of the most

Black bear charges through camp, Neacola Mountains.

rewarding parts of exploring and photographing the Alaska Range. Although sometimes these brushes have been a little too exciting, I would not trade them for an experience void of wildlife. Unfortunately, the Alaska Range is slowly falling victim to the same human pres-sures that we have put on other wilderness areas of the world: industrial mining, overhunting, increasing rec-reational use. These stresses will ultimately lead to the same conclusion: a landscape with few or no wild resi-dents, essentially a pretty place without a soul.

Mount Spurr guards the southern end of the Tordrillo Mountains with Chakachamna and Shamrock lakes in the foreground.

LEFT Caribou cross an unnamed glacier in the Delta Mountains.

RIGHT Strong winds form intricate sastrugi formations in the snow, Delta Mountains.

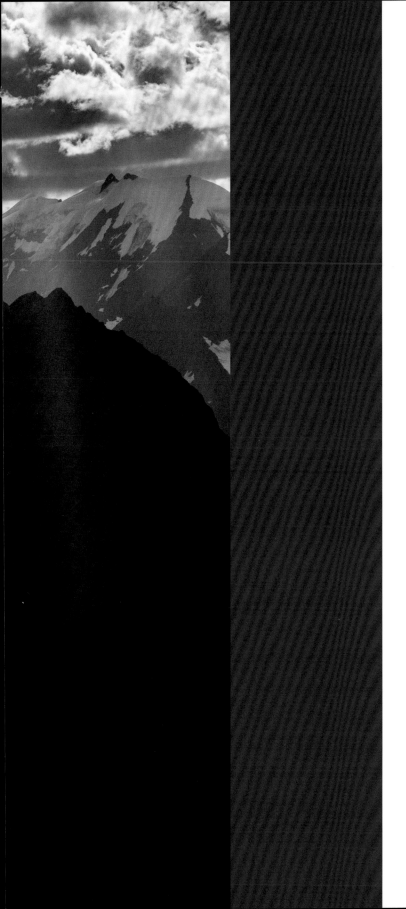

HISTORICAL SUMMITS

BRIAN OKONEK

Looking south from the summit of Denali, Diane and I (along with our team of mountaineering clients) gazed down at glacier-filled valleys cutting through a maze of rugged peaks. There is no higher peak in North America. Thirty miles away, the mountains of the Alaska Range end abruptly and the glaciers terminate, turning to silt-laden rivers. Beyond, the braided rivers disappear into the lush green Susitna River watershed, where detail is lost to the blur of distance. Undetectable was the river's destination: Cook Inlet.

Upon seeing the central Alaska Range from Cook Inlet in 1794, Captain George Vancouver made the first written reference to the dramatic peaks as "distant stupendous mountains covered with snow, and apparently detached from one another." He had seen the two highest mountains in the Range—Denali (20,310 feet, or 6191 meters) and Mount Foraker (17,400

Sunlight streams through developing thunderclouds, Mount Dall and the Dall Glacier, Denali National Park and Preserve.

feet, or 5300 meters)—from the deck of his ship over 130 miles away.

The territory of Alaska was purchased by the United States in 1867. Naturalist and explorer William Healey Dall, who had ascended the Yukon River the year before and noted the huge mountains he had seen to the south, recommended naming them the "Alaskan Range," eventually called the "Alaska Range" by locals. In 1896, gold prospector William Dickey labored to pull his boat against the swift current of the Susitna River. For days he had seen a rugged skyline of peaks coming into finer detail. With incredible accuracy, he estimated that the highest one was about 20,000 feet, which he named Mount McKinley for Ohio politician William McKinley (Dickey's preferred presidential candidate). The name stuck, although in 1980, Mount McKinley National Park was officially changed to the more culturally significant Denali National Park and Preserve. And in 2015 the highest peak was officially renamed Denali.

It wasn't until the gold rush that the US Congress was spurred to finance exploratory expeditions of the territory. Small groups of US Army and US Geological Survey men unraveled the topography of the sparsely mapped Interior. These hard-core naturalists, geologists, and topographers made early accounts of the Alaska Range. Traveling lightly provisioned, they covered huge swaths of uncharted country often on the verge of starvation, harassed by hordes of mosquitoes, their boots rotting off their feet. They mapped the routes Alaska Natives had used for generations to cross the Alaska Range—Mentasta Pass, Isabel Pass, Broad Pass, Simpson Pass, and Rainy Pass. Few other crossings were not blocked by glacier ice. For centuries, Alaska Natives had lived in sight of the huge mountain, surviving off what

LEFT Opie Combs celebrates the warm morning sun below the huge north face of Mount Deborah.

RIGHT Sy Cloud and Chris Wrobel descend through the Kahiltna Icefall with Mount Foraker looming in the background.

the rivers, the forest, and the tundra provided them. They acknowledged the mountain with a variety of names, depending on which tribe they belonged to. The Dena'ina of Upper Cook Inlet referred to it as Dghelay Ka'a (Traleika), to those of the Upper Kuskokwim it was Diinaazi, and the Koyukon called it Diinaalii (Denali)—Big Mountain, the Tall One. A USGS expedition led by Robert Muldrow and George Eldridge in 1898 verified that Denali was indeed North America's highest mountain.

Alfred Brooks's 1902 USGS expedition was the first to document an overland approach to the base of the mountain. His team passed by its north side and traversed from west to east through the future national park. Brooks wrote an article that appeared in *National Geographic* proposing how the mountain might be climbed. The first attempts came quickly. Mountaineering in the Alaska Range had begun.

FOR NEARLY TWO DECADES, my wife, Diane, and I led Denali expeditions, mountaineering seminars, and backpacking trips throughout the central Alaska Range. It has been our backyard, where we have skied, backpacked, climbed, and taken in thousands of sunsets. Drawn by the splendid mountain views, my family built a cabin at the base of the Alaska Range, where the horizon is dominated by Denali and many other mighty peaks. The area has long attracted a broad cross section of people living out the Alaskan dream. Stories of neighbors' mountaineering adventures in the Range sparked my desire as a teen to experience the glacier-carved valleys and wildly sculpted peaks. Seasoned climbers took me under their wing and mentored my alpine apprenticeship. Both of my parents

enthusiastically supported my appetite for adventure. My dad, a skillful pilot, loved flying me and my friends into the Range. I have had the fortunate opportunity to follow routes blazed by the early pioneers and generations of mountaineers and to experience the thrill of breaking the first trail up peaks never before climbed.

The first climbers had to overcome exhausting challenges to reach Denali. It is 130 trailless miles from the coast. Swift glacier rivers flow from the Alaska Range; the valleys are low and thickly carpeted in forest and dense, twisted, almost impenetrable patches of alder and willow. Boggy muskegs and swampy sloughs are numerous. During the short, intense summer, mosquitoes are relentless. Incessant rains brought misery to daily trail life. Men were wet to the bone, flour and beans molded, their precious store of sugar oozed away. Winter travel was defined by short daylight hours, brutal cold, and deep snow. Despite the hardships, the early expeditions explored a tremendous amount of terrain. The entire central Alaska Range was circumnavigated in a vain attempt to unlock the mountain's weaknesses.

Between 1903 and 1912, nine expeditions attempted to reach the summit of Denali. They incorporated pack trains of horses, hand-lined boats up swift rivers, and used early motor-driven river boats or dog teams to overcome the long overland approaches. The glaciers flowing from the Denali Massif were probed from the north and the south in search of a feasible route to the base of Denali, and they intrepidly found a route to the top. These expeditions broke the first crucial trails. A group of gold miners (known as Sourdoughs) from Kantishna were the first to pioneer a climbing route up Denali in the early spring of 1910.

While prospecting and hunting in the foothills, they discovered a way to the summit via the Muldrow Glacier. Dog teams were key. Winter travel, when the rivers and lakes are frozen and the land is covered in snow, is more 'efficient than overland summer travel. Dogs hauled supplies all the way to eleven thousand feet on the glacier, overcoming several big icefalls and countless crevasses. From there the men cut a staircase for thousands of feet up the ice of the northeastern ridge. On April 3, these mountaineers, not versed in modern-day skills, pulled off a remarkable feat of super-human endurance: they ascended Denali's North Peak (19,470 feet, or 5930 meters). They were tough, impeccably abled at winter travel in Alaska's most challenging conditions, and they possessed uncanny common sense. They were not afraid to take risks, calculated or not. They wore homemade crampons on their soft-soled mukluks, they didn't use a safety rope, and they dragged a fourteen-foot spruce pole along with them to hang their flag. The higher South Peak still remained to be climbed, but the route to the upper mountain had been established.

The privilege of reaching Denali's highest summit was that of Archdeacon Hudson Stuck and Harry Karstens, who led a team in 1913 that included Walter Harper and Robert Tatum. Once again, dogs were used to haul supplies to the Muldrow Glacier. The northeastern ridge, which would be named in honor of Karstens, was totally different from what the Sourdough expedition had encountered. A powerful earthquake in 1912 had transformed the ridge from a serpentine arête of smooth snow to a serrated series of teetering ice blocks, ice pinnacles, and crevasses. It took a month for the team to chop a staircase up its treacherous crest to gain access to the upper mountain. They pushed up to 17,600 feet (5360 meters) before placing their final camp on the glacier between the two peaks of Denali that now bears Harper's name. The youngest in the group and half Alaska Native, Harper was the first to summit. Denali was climbed exclusively by this route until 1951.

In 1936, 1937, and 1938, Bradford Washburn photographed the mountain for *National Geographic* by air. Via these flights, he saw what early explorers had missed. At the head of the forty-five-mile long Kahiltna Glacier, the longest in the Alaska Range, was a ridge that offered moderate climbing terrain and low hazards. In 1951 Washburn and his companions pioneered the West Buttress route, which would become the most popular way to climb Denali. While several of the party walked in overland from Wonder Lake, most of the team and equipment was dropped off by airplane. This made it safer, easier, and faster to climb Denali.

After Denali was climbed for a second time in 1932, mountaineers ventured to other summits. The ascent of Mount Foraker came in 1934. Approached in much the same overland style as the pioneer exploratory expeditions, it was a technically more difficult climb than Karstens Ridge. Eventually each of Foraker's ridges was climbed. In 1977 the seasoned team of George Lowe and Michael Kennedy pushed new boundaries of alpine climbing in Alaska when they climbed the extremely technical south face of Mount Foraker up the Infinite Spur. From the Kahiltna Glacier, Foraker's northeast ridge forms the divide of the Alaska Range. I recall my first winter ascent of this route, years ago. Storms pounded the mountain, forcing us to wait in snow caves for days on end. No other climbing expeditions were in the Range then.

Mountains reflected in an unnamed tarn above the Ruth Glacier, Denali National Park and Preserve

For one of my partners, alpinist Dave Johnston, this was routine. He had made the first winter ascent of Denali in 1967. While descending from the summit, he, Art Davidson, and Ray Genet had been caught in a severe wind storm; they were forced to spend six days in a tiny snow cave with inadequate food or fuel. Dave named our ascent route on Mount Foraker "Sultana Ridge" in honor of the Native name that means Denali's wife. Lieutenant Herron of the US Army named Mount Foraker in 1899, when he led an expedition across the Alaska Range west of the Kichatna Spires. Herron and his men were saved from starvation by the Alaska Natives of Telida on the northwest side of the Range.

The possibilities for mountaineering expanded in 1954, a pivotal year in the Alaska Range. American climber Fred Beckey stormed the Range with one of the finest climbing seasons ever recorded. He was a member of a team that first climbed the Northwest Buttress of Denali's North Peak. A little over a month later, along with two companions, he made the first ascent of Mount Hunter (14,573 feet, or 4442 meters), the third highest peak in the Alaska Range, via the West Ridge. Before the summer's end the same trio, which included Henry Meybohm and Heinrich Harrer, who had made the first ascent of the fearsome north face of Switzerland's Eiger, climbed the showy Mount Deborah (12,339 feet, or 3761 meters) in the eastern Alaska Range. First ascents reached a feverish pace in the 1960s. Iconic peaks patterned with hanging glaciers, etched by knife-edge cornice-draped ridges with sheer arêtes of granite, line the multiple glaciers of the Denali Massif. One by one each summit was attained.

THE VAST MAJORITY OF THE approximately twelve hundred people who now attempt to climb Denali each year do so via the West Buttress. About half of them succeed. Because there are currently dozens of routes up the mountain of varying difficulty levels, Denali has an irresistible draw for mountaineers from around the world. It's huge geologic uplift, towering above the lowlands surrounding it, its topographic location striding between the Gulf of Alaska and the Interior, and its northern latitude of 63 degrees make for cold temperatures and powerful storms. By even the least difficult route, Denali remains a major mountaineering challenge. An average of four or five camps are placed above base camp, with high camp established at 17,300 feet (about 5270 meters). It is a mountaineer's route with sections of steep snow and ice to climb but

no extremely technical terrain. This does not make it an easy climb, however. This world-class, three-week expedition includes cold temperatures, high altitude, and monumental storms as well as the challenges of shouldering heavy packs, living in cramped spaces, and building fortifying wind walls.

Now leading a hardy group of climbers on their first Denali summit, Diane and I break trail up the broad expanse of the Kahiltna Glacier. The three loftiest summits of the Alaska Range rise abruptly above the ice-filled valley: Denali, Mount Foraker, and Mount Hunter. Airplanes have long superseded arduous overland approaches. A squadron of ski-equipped aircraft come and go, delivering mountaineers to base camp. We plan to ascend the West Buttress and descend Karstens Ridge. It will be a traverse of the Alaska Range via the highest summit: a mountaineering odyssey that has few parallels. As we ascend the Kahiltna Glacier, we pass underneath Mount Frances (10,450 feet, or 3185 meters), Mount Crosson (12,352 feet, or 3765 meters), the West Kahiltna Peak (12,835 feet, or 3912 meters)— all worthy climbs in their own right. They attract little attention, however, being overshadowed by Denali.

From the confluence of the Northeast Fork of the Kahiltna Glacier, the two-mile uplift of Denali's south face is fully visible. Pink granite and blue ice rise dramatically above the glacier's shattered surface. An all-star team led by the renowned Italian alpinist Ricardo Cassin broke new barriers in difficulties when they climbed directly up the center of the face in 1961. The Cassin Ridge remains a classic Alaska Range test-piece. At eleven thousand feet, we were finally on the flank of Denali. We could see beyond the terminus of the glaciers to the northwest to the tundra ponds far below.

LEFT, TOP Seracs and crevasses, Triumvirate Glacier, Tordrillo Mountains **BOTTOM** A boulder takes a ride on the Tatina Glacier, Kichatna Mountains, Denali National Park and Preserve.

RIGHT Endless ridges and nameless summits lead to the Mooses Tooth and Broken Tooth, Denali National Park and Preserve.

The early explorers took fifty days to reach the mountain across that expanse.

Summer storms deliver huge amounts of snow here along the divide of the Alaska Range: food for the glaciers and the source of disorienting whiteouts and heavy trail-breaking for climbers. Diane and I climbed with our clients using ropes to protect us from the possibility of falling into a crevasse. We used crampons and ice axes to give us sure footing on the icy slopes. On steep headwalls and the exposed narrow ridge of the West Buttress, we safeguarded our movements with fixed lines and belays. Although self-sufficient, our climbing party was not alone. We leap-frogged up the mountain with other groups, camped near other teams, and occasionally communicated with the outside world by CB radio.

Dragging our sleds around Windy Corner and into the flat basin at 14,300 feet (4360 meters) was like coming home. Diane and I had spent two summers here working for a high-altitude research project. At times the facility served as an emergency ward. Horrible injuries received in falls, frostbitten extremities that left victims immobilized, and life-threatening high-altitude illnesses were tended to here until weather allowed for an evacuation. By the time we reached the West Buttress high camp at 17,300 feet (5270 meters), the scenery was like viewing the world from an airliner. We relayed loads of food and fuel to Denali Pass (18,200 feet, or 5547 meters) and established our high camp on the Harper Glacier, where the first ascent of Denali had taken place. After cutting a tent platform in the hard wind-packed snow, we sawed snow blocks for wind walls to shelter our tents. We were exactly where the Stuck and Karstens expedition had set up their tent. As isolated as a person could get from civilization, they must have felt like they were on the moon. We were insignificant between Denali's two peaks. Climbers bound for the summit were but specks upon the vastness of the upper mountain.

SUNSET PASTELS PAINTED THE RANGE at midnight. No darkness enveloped the night. Midsummer sunrise colors of glowing pink saturated the summit at 3:00 a.m. We moved slowly, groggy from fatigue and altitude. I savored the flush of the morning's first hot drink, relished another and another. Far to the east the fin-like silhouettes of Mount Deborah, Hess Mountain (11,940 feet, or 3639 meters), and Mount Hayes (13,832 feet, or 4216 meters) caught the light. Hayes had first been climbed by a team that included Bradford and Barbara Washburn. In 1947, Barbara was the first woman to stand on both peaks of Denali. Brad was the first person to ascend many other peaks now visible from our vantage point. Famous for his masterful large-format black-and-white photographs that captured the alpine splendor of the Alaska Range, he also produced an artistic detailed map of the Denali Massif. Many new climbs still begin with dreams inspired by Brad's sweeping photography.

The Alaska Range forms a barrier between the coast and the Interior. Often a sea of clouds obscures the lowlands on one side or the other, dammed by the many mountains. Blizzards commonly blow across the ridges with unrelenting force. This time, Diane and I had a perfect day to summit. It was calm and clear. I had climbed Denali for the first time from this very camp when I was a senior in high school. After many climbs to the summit since then, I am still filled with nervous anticipation. With each expedition, with a fresh group of excited climbers, my experiences accumulate like

the annual lines of snowfall revealed in the wall of a crevasse. Stepping onto the summit, I see the south side of the Denali Massif spread out below us. The Ruth Glacier's multiple tributaries gathered in the Don Sheldon Amphitheater before exiting toward the lowlands through the Gateway and into the Great Gorge. In 1906 and 1910 the first attempts on Denali from the south approached the mountain through this ice-filled gorge.

Barely distinguishable among the hundreds of summits and pinnacles was a tiny rock outcrop made infamous by Dr. Frederick Cook's photograph of his partner, Edward Barrill, holding a flag at its top. The caption indicated this was the summit of North America, but Belmore Browne and Herschel Parker located

that very spot in 1910, proving Cook's claim a total hoax. Browne and Parker spent fifty days on the Ruth Glacier searching for a route to Denali's summit, to no avail. Unstable icefalls and avalanche slopes confronted them at every turn. The ridges they attempted would not be climbed for many years. The South Buttress was not ascended until 1954. That expedition went on to do the first traverse of Denali. Elton Thayer, the leader of the group, was killed in a fall while descending Karstens Ridge. The East Buttress was climbed in the 1960s. The hazards of icefalls and tedious corniced ridges have left that route seldom climbed.

The Ruth Glacier is lined with technically demanding, iconic peaks offering no easy way to their summits.

The French, led by Lionel Terray, were the first to ascend Mount Huntington (12,240 feet, or 3730 meters), in 1964. Razor ridges draped in cornices and sheer granite faces make Huntington an enticing mountain, and desperate struggles have played out on its steep terrain. It continues to be a magnet for elite climbers from around the world. The same summer, a German team climbed the massive bulk of the Mooses Tooth (10,330 feet, or 3139 meters), a wonderfully apt name for this peak. Climbers crisscrossed the Range, seeking out first ascents and new routes. The first big wall climb in the Alaska Range came in 1974. David Roberts, Galen Rowell, and Ed Ward ascended the mile-high southeast face of Mount Dickey (9545 feet, or 2909 meters). Pitch after pitch, they worked a line up the massive granite face, marveling at the colorful flowers that blossomed on the ledges. Roberts had been on the first ascent of the Wickersham Wall, Denali's north face, in 1963. Two years later, he upped the ante with a magnificent ascent of Mount Huntington's west face.

From the summit of Denali, Diane and I studied terrain that came into sharper focus with each ascent. We noticed details unseen on earlier expeditions. Our clients were overwhelmed. There was too much of a view to comprehend it all. Far to the west beyond Mount Foraker, the Kichatna Spires, a group of a sharp, granite towers, jut out of narrow glaciated valleys. These peaks are demanding and the weather notoriously bad. Diane and I had once hiked through the spires on a busman's holiday. Low, misty clouds raced through the peaks and a cold rain beat down. The rock and ice was raw, inhospitable in the fog. Herds of Dall sheep grazed in tiny meadows at the toe of a glacier.

At Simpson Pass, where Lieutenant Herron had found passage across the Range, we stumbled upon a wolf den. Curious pups eyed us as we crawled into our tent to watch them. Another day's walk through hills saturated in autumn colors brought us to Rainy Pass. Everything looked cheerier in the sun. New snow covered all the summits. Alfred Brooks crossed the Range here in 1902. Today the longest sled dog race in the world crosses the Alaska Range through Rainy Pass following the historic Iditarod Trail.

DIANE AND I DID ONE LAST ROTATION, gazing from the summit. To the south, just beyond the mountains, we could see the lake where we had first met, and our family cabin is tucked among the spruce and birch. It was time to return to a more hospitable environment. Our group descended by the route from which Denali was first climbed. Few mountaineers ascend this route each season, and we encountered only one other team during the six days it took to walk to Wonder Lake. As we climbed down the Harper Glacier, we felt isolated from the forested lowlands far below. The slightest breeze had a cold, penetrating bite. It was not conducive to taking breaks. The rock-hard, cold snow squeaked under the thrust of our ice axes and crampon points. Snow bridges echoed hollowly. It was a mine field of crevasses. Cornices curled into the darkness of sinister holes. Ice seracs, like prows of ships, rose above the glacier pushed by unseen forces. Wind-sculpted sastrugi formations patterned the surface of the glacier. Pink granite towered above. The sky was the darkest blue imaginable.

Between two icefalls we could see the lonely spot where Browne and Parker had placed their high camp in 1912. Despite their disappointment in not reaching the top, they were happy to finally descend from the unrelenting cold for the good life of the lowlands. They had begun their journey at the coastal town of Seward. It had taken three months for the team to travel by dogsled to Denali. Continuing down, our team passed the Sourdough Gully, where the 1910 expedition had made a steep ascent to the North Peak. Climbing the gully would be a serious endeavor even with modern gear and techniques.

My favorite camp on the mountain is among the granite boulders jutting out of the ice below Browne Tower at 14,530 feet (4430 meters). Our dome tent fit nicely at the base of the same rock where Stuck and Karstens had erected their tiny canvas wall tent. The granite offers a security not felt on the crevassed surface of the glaciers. The mountain drops steeply, opening up a long view to the north and east of the Alaska Range. The solstice sun shines for more than twenty hours a day. Compared to the frigid winds of the Harper Glacier, it is paradise. Stuck left a thermometer here that when recovered nearly twenty years later had recorded a low of -95°F (-71°C). On the ascent many people in our group began to feel the effects of the rarified air at this elevation. After living high on the mountain for over a week, the air now felt thick and rich, the worries of altitude sickness no longer a concern.

We advanced down the airy crest of Karstens Ridge. The exposure is breathtaking. This ridge was the key to gaining the upper ramparts of Denali and its two peaks for the early pioneer climbers. And it was vital for our group of climbers to get off Denali. Steep sections could easily end in disaster. Conditions ranged from thigh-deep snow to hard wind-battered snow that our

Alpenglow on Hess Mountain, Hayes Range

crampons barely cut into. The contours of the ridge were smooth, as earlier expeditions had found them. No other parties have had to contend with the horrendous, jumbled ice blocks that Stuck and Karstens had to overcome. Even so, we placed sections of fixed lines to safeguard our movements as we downclimbed.

At eleven thousand feet we entered the confined valley of the Muldrow Glacier. Hanging glaciers tilt down from everywhere. A maze of crevasses define the Great Icefall, the Hill of Cracks, and the Lower Icefall. Negotiating questionable snow bridges and keeping out of the reach of avalanches was nerve-racking. It was hard to imagine what ascending this glacier with dog teams had been like for the early expeditions. On my first trip through the Great Icefall, years ago, I had earned a great respect for crevasses, when I had dangled at the end of the climbing rope, swinging above the blackness of a

crevasse bottom. A luminous light filtered through the snow bridge above me where a tiny hole had pierced it, marking my fall through. The rope (and the partners I was tied to) had saved me from plummeting farther.

ON OUR TWENTY-THIRD DAY INTO the expedition, Diane and I and our trail-hardened clients stepped from glacier ice to the lateral moraine of the Muldrow Glacier. We no longer had to travel roped up. We returned to a world of vivid colors, scents, and sounds. Water trickled down through patches of green moss, and bright pink alpine flowers splashed the stones with color. Marmots whistled and song birds flitted about. We had been liberated from the land of snow and ice, a magical transition. There were still miles of tundra to walk across and fast rivers to ford, but we were home, where people have survived for thousands of years.

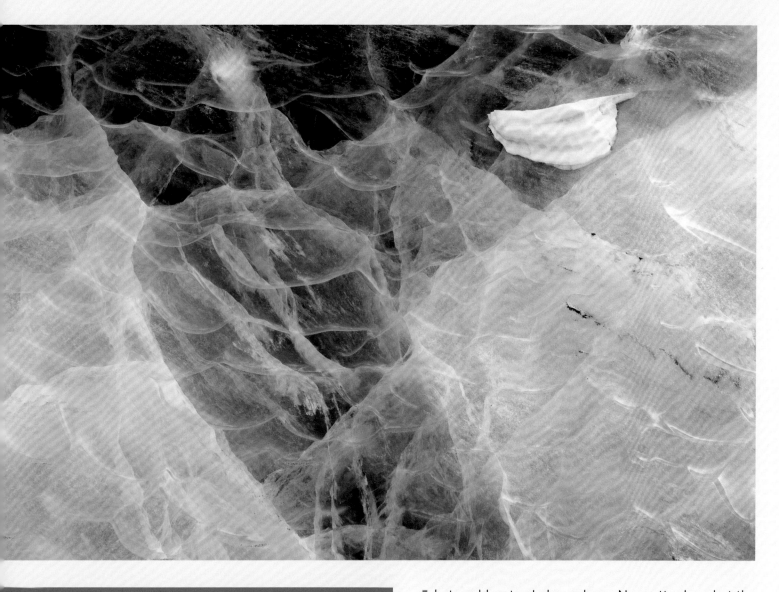

Old, dense transparent ice, Black Rapids Glacier, Hayes Range

PHOTOGRAPHING THE ALASKA RANGE
RIVERS OF WATER AND ICE
CARL BATTREALL

I hate cold water. I always have. No matter how hot the outside temperature is, I loathe cold swimming pools and swimming holes. When I moved to Alaska, my dislike of cold water intensified. Possibly the most hazardous thing in the state, more dangerous than bears or avalanches, frigid water is an unforgiving killer. I swore to avoid it as much as possible.

And I had, until now. We were a group of four, on a two-week, fifty-mile glacier traverse of the Neacola Mountains in the southwestern corner of the Alaska Range. On our second day we came to a glacial river that needed to be forded. It was typical July weather, dark and rainy. The rivers had swollen after weeks of constant precipitation. After multiple attempts to cross in different locations, we were shivering. My feet were lifeless bricks; the cold had sucked all feeling from them.

Finally we found a decent spot to cross, ten feet wide but moving fast. Quickly, we set up a pack line: Andy, then Patrick, with Colin and me at the tail. "Left, right, left, right!" Andy commanded. I kept my head down, swearing to myself that I wouldn't swim. I held onto Colin's pack, pulling it down, keeping him from floating away. We were hardly moving. The boiling water was rising higher up Andy's body, nearing his naval. Colin and I were shaking. In slow motion, Andy went under. Then Patrick. Six foot four and 250 pounds, gone. Colin and I held our ground, but it was useless. Down went Colin. Screaming, I realized I was going to die, via cold water. I was pulled under.

Proper river-swimming protocol with a backpack goes like this: Unbuckle your hipbelt and sternum strap before crossing. Take your pack off and sit feet up, facing downriver. Use one arm to paddle to shore, the other arm to hold onto your pack. Rolling sideways down the river, like a big rock, I was in the proper position alright: the proper position to drown. Underwater then above, under then above, I called for help each time my head was up. Stupidly, I had kept my sternum strap on. I tried to unsnap it while rolling, but my hands were unresponsive. I was panicking.

Shut up, Carl—no one is going to save you. Save yourself, I told myself. After I struggled to point myself downriver, I realized I was floating near the shore. I flipped, swam like hell, and clawed the bank. I made it.

NOT ALL EXPEDITIONS GO AS planned. That is the single scariest experience I have had in my fifteen years as a professional mountain photographer and explorer. In the end we were all fine. I broke two toes, sprained a wrist, and bruised my ego. Alaska's rivers are notorious for abruptly ending adventures; even groups of hardy, experienced mountain travelers get shut down. The massive glaciers that descend from the glorious mountains are the source of the majority of the Alaska Range's rivers. As these glaciers slither down the mountains, they crush and grind the underlying rock, creating thick, brown flour. This pulverized rock, or glacial silt, rushes out of the underbelly of the frozen beasts in a milky torrent. These silt-laden rivers are very tricky to cross because you can't see the bottom. The depths are very deceiving: a huge braid may be only ankle deep, while a small, three-foot-wide channel could be over your waist. You won't know the true depth until you are halfway across.

The other issue is that the sides and bottom of the rivers are in a continual state of transformation. The silt does not allow for stability. Rocks are always shifting and can often be heard rolling in the water, unseen. During that fateful crossing, our ford across literally reshaped the river. New braids formed, and the channel we had our trouble in split into three variations.

Yes, I despise glacial rivers, but my fascination with their source—the glaciers—borders on obsession. The glaciers of Alaska and the Alaska Range are simply awe-inspiring. They can be gentle giants, meandering through the tundra, or wicked, fractured icefalls that impossibly defy gravity as they cling to vertical cliffs. A glacier is also a river, a frozen, slow-moving one. Gravity and the water that travels under the glacier allow it to slide, twisting around mountains, pouring over cliffs as great icefalls. Strange formations created by wind and the endless summer sun dazzle and amaze. Twisted turquoise streams rush into inviting pools or into frightening holes that drop into the glacier's belly. Each glacier has a unique character created by its environment. Weather, terrain, and gravity mold a glacier's personality. Some are dirty, aggressive, and destructive; others are gentle and contemplative. They are all beautiful.

More than just a fun phenomenon to explore and photograph, glaciers are a frozen trail for the mountain explorer. All the big mountains of the Alaska Range are glaciated, and glacier travel is required if you wish to visit them up close. Many of the Alaska Range glaciers are riddled with gaping crevasses. The only way to cross them is during the late winter and spring, when the crevasses are packed with deep snow and the rivers are frozen. Many areas of the Alaska Range can really only be visited during the snowy months. Traveling via skis, a person can cover great distances using the rivers and glaciers as trails.

One of my more memorable glacier trips was on the mighty Kahiltna Glacier. Descending forty-four miles, beginning at Kahiltna Pass on the west flank of Denali, it is the longest glacier in the Alaska Range. Its northeast fork is the home of Denali base camp and the overpopulated West Buttress route. During the climbing season (May through mid-July), hundreds of tents litter the landscapes. I have never had an interest in climbing Denali, but I have always wanted to go to the Kahiltna Glacier, which squeezes its way between the Alaska Range's three tallest mountains: Denali, Foraker, and Hunter—some the best mountain scenery on Earth.

I figured the only way to get a true wilderness experience on the Kahiltna was to go there in March, when it is empty. I convinced my partner in mountain crime, Sy, and our good friend Chris to try and ski the length of the Kahiltna Glacier in March. We would have the mountain sanctuary to ourselves, but we would pay the price for our solitude. A wicked storm trapped us in a miserable whiteout, delivering deep snow and high avalanche conditions on the lower part of the glacier. Freezing wind forced us to cover every part of our bodies at all times.

But the most challenging weather came after the storm. It was our first clear day of the trip and the sun felt like a gift from the mountain gods. As if we had gotten a shot of Prozac, our mood changed, our spirits soared. Dazzled by the incredible mountains that loomed all around us, we were not prepared when the sun gently dropped behind Mount Foraker. Like a match being snuffed, when the last ray of sun vanished from the mountainside, a harsh reality set in. Our thermometer read -20°F (-29°C). *Brrr.* Soon the temperature was -30°F(-34°C). Armed with two hot water bottles, I climbed into my icy sleeping bag. Before Chris crawled into his bag, he looked one last time at the thermometer: it had reached the bottom, -40°F (-40°C). Chris tried to read but his book was too cold to hold, even with his down mitts on.

I knew the next morning would be spectacular, clear with Foraker basking in the rising sunlight. But I couldn't get up, it was just too cold. Chris and Sy mocked me: "What kind of a mountain photographer are you?" I wondered, *Am I tough enough to do this?* We broke camp after the sun had thawed us. Temperatures would improve as we descended the glacier.

The following year I returned to the Alaska Range again in March, but I couldn't convince Sy or Chris to join me. The memory of the cold was still too fresh.

In the summer months and in the early fall, glaciers offer a reprieve from the thick, relentless brush of the mountainside. They can allow quick travel through otherwise miserable terrain. Unfortunately, as the glaciers of the Alaska Range retreat with alarming speed, they become more and more difficult to access. The "green line," as I call the brush line, chases after the glaciers as they cower farther up the valleys. The glacial silt and newly exposed soil are extremely fertile, and growth happens quicker than you would expect in such a northern latitude. Many of the large glaciers that were used by Alaska's early explorers have retreated ten or twenty miles back into the mountains. And because the Alaska Range is primarily a trailfree wilderness, that can mean miles upon miles of bushwhacking to reach the glaciers and their mountain arena.

From Patagonia to Yosemite, glaciers have shaped and carved the mountain landscapes we know and love. The world's glaciers are a stockpile of freshwater. As they melt, the ocean levels rise, threatening to devour islands and shorelines around the world. With many mountain regions becoming drier and receiving less annual snowfall, glaciers could become a vital source for freshwater, but they are vanishing quickly. Mountain glaciers may only hold 1 percent of the world's glacial ice but contribute 30 percent to sea level rise. As reported in the *Alaska Dispatch News,* a study published in the July 2015 issue of *Geophysical Research Letters* found that Alaska contains 11 percent of the world's mountain glaciers, and Alaska's glaciers lose approximately seventy-five billion tons of ice each year (the majority of that loss is from mountain glaciers). The water that pours from their base has and continues to be the life source for Alaska, but what about the world's glaciers? Every few years, politicians and entrepreneurs joke about building a water pipeline from Alaska to the Lower 48.

As ridiculous as that sounds, the joke becomes less humorous with each passing year, especially since much of the western United States is in a constant state of drought, with wildfires raging six months a year. According to Yereth Rosen, of the *Alaska Dispatch News,* Alaska's glaciers produce enough water annually to fill thirty million Olympic-size swimming pools. That could irrigate a lot of crops and lessen the burden of the West's tortured rivers and lakes.

The melting of the world's glaciers affects us all. We must consider the changes of our warming world in a global way. What is happening in our own backyard, the decisions we make locally, could be affecting people a thousand miles away.

LEFT Mount Barrille and its shadow, Ruth Gorge, Denali National Park and Preserve

RIGHT Rivers thick with glacial silt pour into Chakachamna Lake, creating a splendid turquoise color, Tordrillo Mountains.

In a clearing storm on Denali, both the south and north summits are visible, Denali National Park and Preserve.

IMPOSSIBLE IS JUST A WORD
MODERN CLIMBING IN THE ALASKA RANGE

CLINT HELANDER

Boreal spruce forests and muskeg blanketed by winter snows blurred beneath us like frozen waves. Our tiny plane bucked in downdrafts created by the turmoil of air over distant glaciers. Life-sustaining hills evolved into jagged forms, born of violent tectonic uplift and etched by glacial torrents. The Alaska Range's colossal monoliths of ice and stone grew in a slow crescendo through the windshield. Wingtips veered perilously close to arching buttresses. The plane's engine roared into high rpms as we climbed through thinning air.

Fall lasts only a few weeks in the Alaska Range. Photographing the brilliant colors is difficult because snow often covers them when they are at their prime, Denali National Park and Preserve.

A sense of vertigo lightened my heavy muscles as the plane slowed to a stalling speed. After a smooth landing on specially designed skis, we floated to a stop in deep powder. Duffle bags stuffed with three weeks of supplies formed a colorful oasis amid the stark blue and white glacier. The departing plane's high-pitched drone echoed, then faded to magnificent silence. We strained to hear any noise over our own breathing. In every direction around Denali the biggest mountains I had ever seen rose above me.

This is impossible, I thought. The mountain walls told ancient stories in cacophonies of shattering force, energy exuding in seamless forms. Depressions and flow lines had been etched by eons of cascading meltwater. Energy paused in the questioning silence and stirred awake with the wind. I marveled at the frozen chaos of an ice cliff precariously hanging thousands of feet above my camp. In the rumbling Ruth Glacier, I sensed a force continuously contracting and releasing. Somewhere amid its compressing ice, the body of the great Alaskan solo climber John Waterman is forever entombed. Ever present and ever changing, this energy was sometimes comforting, as the first rays of sun warmed a shadowed, glacial hollow. Other times it bred fear, as hurricane-force winds stretched the limits of a tent in a -50°F (-46°C) storm.

PERSPECTIVE IS EVERYTHING. A near ridge seems incomprehensibly large until compared to its greater surroundings. From high above, it is as indistinguishable as a single fleck of feldspar on a sprawling granite wall. A goal is unreachable until broken into its many parts, like jumping widespread rocks to reach the far side of a raging river. As an eager eighteen-year-old, I began hiking the local summits of Anchorage's Chugach front range. Older college friends taught me to ice climb on roadside glaciers. I honed my winter survival skills during December camping trips in the mountains, with the glow of city lights permeating the skyline. Every book and scrap of literature I could find on climbing in the Alaska Range lined my bookshelf. Clinging to my experienced cohorts, I listened to their tales of climbing Denali and other difficult peaks in the Alaska Range. They were brash, rebellious, and confident. I longed to join the ranks of these counterculture demigods. At last, over several cases of beer on a dark Alaskan winter night, I convinced one of them to join me on my first trip to the big mountains.

On a crystal-cold morning, my synapses fired nervously as the tiny plane taxied down the Talkeetna runway for the icy peaks that had filled my dreams. In early March the Alaska Range was a humanless spectacle of confining shadows interlacing a multitude of chilling hues that bathed towering peaks. I avoided looking at the thermometer. As we chopped blocks to fortify camp in wind-compacted snow, our shovels creaked and strained. The sun traversed out of sight behind Mount Huntington, its weak beams shimmering high above in purple flares. A ghostly breeze stung my face. The surrounding mountains lurked behind morphing shrouds of mist. We donned goggles and shielded

our faces under jackets against penetrating gusts. At last we had a bastion of blocked walls to cower against the wind. Within minutes, though, they were blown in, our safety zone indistinguishable against the expanding miles of featureless whiteness.

The evening's darkness brought a cutting wind. We scurried into our down jackets and retreated to our cramped tent and massive sleeping bags. Our focus momentarily waned from the increasing storm outside to the sputtering roar and radiating warmth of the white gas stove. Minutes passed in what felt like days, one page of a book at a time. I burrowed deeper in my bag as the tent walls sagged against the weight of wind-blown snow. I traced my breaths as they condensed into frost feathers that hung above my head like doubts in crystalline form.

At dawn, an orb of radiating light beamed through the tent fabric. Distant avalanches resonated like drawn-out Gregorian chants. We unzipped our tent and emerged to a world of snow-white purity. Clouds evaporated, and I winced as blinding sunlight reflected off the pearly surroundings. My heart raced with fear intertwined with awe. My partner, Seth Holden, a veteran of many expeditions, exuded a stoic calmness. We stared up at the sinuous southwest ridge of Peak 11,300, an offshoot mountain east of Denali. I pondered why this popular peak, which was surrounded by mountains with lively names such as the Mooses Tooth and the Roosters Comb, was identified by a simple elevation number.

After a day of allowing the snow to settle, we loaded our backpacks and prepared to depart in the tantalizing predawn darkness. Firm snow groaned under my boots as I paced around the dug-out kitchen. With gloved hands, I nervously cradled a warm mug of coffee. The next hot drink would be many hours and thousands of vertical feet from this moment. My mind cycled through the lessons Seth had taught me as I sipped the last warm ounce.

Heavily-laden packs cut into our shoulders as we skied away from camp, navigating around gaping crevasses to the shadowed mass looming above. Trenching through waist-deep snow warmed me for the first time in days. Seth climbed up and out of sight, and I willed the rope to move as I danced in place to stave off the cold. Twelve hours of climbing brought us little gain. That night we hid under a rock and huddled together in our -25°F-rated sleeping bags. In the morning I backed off a moderate section and Seth led it with ease. I strived to redeem myself by pushing through fear to lead the next difficult section. Pale shadows encapsulated us in chilling darkness. Soon we realized that deep snow had slowed us too much to reach the distant summit in our scheduled timeframe.

After another frigid night, a day of rappels deposited us on the glacier. Despite the failure, at twenty-two years old, I was gratified by this first significant experience in one of the world's greater ranges. The flight back to Talkeetna took us through the Ruth Gorge, a magnificent canyon of mile-high walls towering above four thousand feet of ice. I saw them a little differently than I had on the flight in. What was before a vast landscape of impossibility now seemed ever so slightly more plausible.

UNTIL THE 1960S, THE ALASKA RANGE was largely unexplored. Fifty-five years later, almost every corner of this natural palette has been painted with experience.

Sy Cloud admires the epic vertical arena that surrounds him, Monolith Pass, Kichatna Mountains.

LEFT Moraine-covered Ruth Glacier, Denali National Park and Preserve

RIGHT, TOP Bending crevasses, Capps Glacier, Tordrillo Mountains BOTTOM Strange moraine-covered serac, lower Ruth Glacier, Denali National Park and Preserve

Early climbs followed natural lines, a gradual sloping face or broad ridge. Most expeditions took place in June, July, and August to avoid the coldest temperatures. Climbing at high altitudes during the colder spring months was thought to be nearly impossible. Expedition climbing or "siege tactics" (moving up the mountain slowly with a large amount of supplies) was standard until the late 1970s. Large teams utilized a division of labor and provided safety in numbers. Members ferried loads to higher camps, installing hundreds and sometimes thousands of feet of fixed rope over the most perilous sections before returning lower to rest and acclimatize.

Stores of supplies allowed teams to wait out stretches of bad weather or quickly retreat if disaster struck. Once acclimatized, they moved higher and repeated the process again and again. To navigate ice up to angles of sixty degrees, climbers chopped hundreds of steps. Expedition-style climbing was the only conceivable method to succeed on such large peaks, but it often subjected teams to higher levels of exposure in dangerous areas. Groups may have to travel under avalanche zones and crevasse fields multiple times. These methods also often left a lot of garbage on otherwise pristine mountains. Decades after their first ascent, many routes are still littered with hundreds of feet of tattered rope.

In 1954, after already completing the first ascent of Denali's Northwest Buttress and Mount Deborah (12,339 feet, or 3761 meters) in the eastern Alaska Range, Fred Beckey and Henry Meybohm joined with Heinrich Harrer. A legendary Austrian mountaineer, Harrer made the first ascent of the Eiger's north face in Switzerland in 1938 and early attempts on Nanga Parbat (26,660 feet, or 8108 meters) in the Himalaya. This

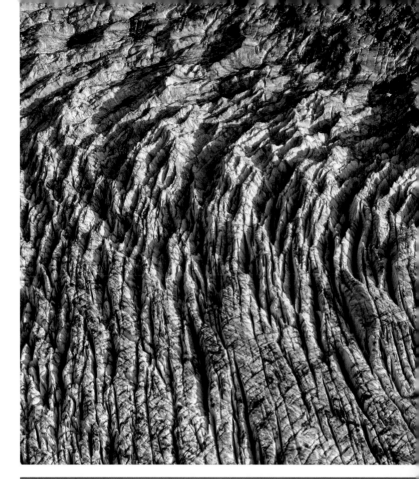

spirited team took a revolutionary approach to the high Alaskan peaks already being employed in the French and Swiss Alps. By climbing "alpine style" (without ferrying loads, using fixed ropes, or in large groups), they could move light and fast in a continual upward progression. Having gained confidence on their previous endeavors, the three men made the unprecedented first ascent of Mount Hunter (14,573 feet, or 4442 meters) in five days via its extremely corniced, three-mile-long west ridge. This single climb heralded in a new acceptance of what was possible upon the continent's most technical subarctic peaks. Their climb is still regarded as one of the most impressive first ascents ever completed

in Alaska. To this day, teams struggle to better the time of the 1954 pioneering team.

With the giants of the central Alaska Range all climbed, teams turned their attention to the shorter and more remote peaks. What they lacked in colossal height, they made up for in extreme technicality. In 1965 the brilliant French alpinist Lionel Terray landed in the West Fork of the Ruth Glacier, drawn there by the mountain profile photographs of Bradford Washburn. Terray had made the first ascent of Makalu (27,838 feet, or 8485 meters) in the Himalaya and Fitz Roy in Patagonia. In Alaska his team fixed ropes over endless cornices and vertical ice on the northwest ridge

to make the audacious first ascent of Mount Huntington (12,241 foot, or 3731 meters). Only a year later, four Harvard students—David Roberts, Matt Hale, Don Jensen, and Ed Bernd—spent forty-one days pioneering the imposing Harvard Route on the concave west face. It was perhaps the most technical route completed in Alaska at the time. Their success was marred by tragedy when Bernd fell to his death on the descent, just one pitch above the end of the technical climbing. His body has never been found.

Climbing in the Alaska Range takes an intense amount of preparation, determination, and luck. The magnitude of even the small peaks is difficult to comprehend. Almost every mountain involves extensive glacier travel, a gauntlet of avalanche or rock fall hazard, rapidly changing weather patterns, and tedious routefinding. And then there is the cold. More so than the tallest Himalayan peaks or even the high summits of Antarctica, the deep freeze of Alaska's mountains has long been respected and feared. Because of its height and latitude, Denali is known as the "coldest mountain in the world." On the first winter ascent in 1967, Art Davidson, Ray Genet, and Dave Johnston desperately clung to life in a snow cave at eighteen thousand feet during a weeklong storm. It was later calculated that they endured windchill values of -148°F (-100°C).

Spring and summer temperatures fare better, but higher camps on the mountain frequently plunge to -50°F (-46°C) for days or weeks at a time.

Primitive equipment was often homemade, cumbersome, and heavy. Early ropes were suspect in strength. Protection consisted of European-imported pitons, rudimentary ice screws, and snow pickets. Technological advancements in gear slowly permitted climbers to move faster and carry less. Hollow ice screws, rigid crampons, and ice axes with recurved picks were popularized throughout the 1970s, allowing climbers to confront the steepest of ice with great security. New creations in rock gear (such as hexes, nuts, and camming devices) made technical ground easier to protect and promoted a fast and light style of climbing.

Today's lightweight clothing and hardware, precise weather forecasts, and extreme training has upped the ante even further. Elite climbers build off of the climbs that inspired them and push the limits, redefining the possibilities once again. Mount Huntington has over a dozen ingenious lines established in a minimalist style. The Harvard Route has been climbed in under twenty-four hours, round-trip. The West Face Couloir, a swath of unrelentingly steep ice, has even been soloed. Denali has been climbed round-trip in under twelve hours and soloed in the winter. Two of its most difficult and largest lines, the Isis Face and the Slovak Direct, have been linked to form a 16,000-foot enchainment that redefined the limits of technical endurance and vision in the modern era.

AS A YOUNG CLIMBER, I idolized alpine visionaries like David Roberts, Art Davidson, Jack Tackle, and John Waterman. In their time they established some of the most exemplary climbs ever completed in Alaska. Waterman's 145-day solo first ascent of Mount Hunter's Southeast Spur teeters on the verge of madness as much today as it did in 1978. As my alpine tutelage continued, I longed to adhere to the cutting-edge style of modern alpinists like Steve House, Mark Westman, Mark Twight, and Colin Haley. By the time he was twenty-two, Haley had completed an astonishingly difficult first ascent of the Entropy Wall (7500 feet, or 2300 meters) in the Hayes Range and the first winter ascent of Mount Huntington, and repeated the seldom-climbed Denali Diamond (7800 feet, or 2380 meters) in forty-six hours.

For some climbers, establishing first ascents is a preeminent goal. Climbers have long relied on photographers and writers to kindle inspiration. Generations have studied Bradford Washburn's timeless black-and-white aerial photographs to spy future first ascents in Alaska and the Yukon. With little more than a single picture or a writer's few words, climbers have traveled across the globe to attempt a mountain they have never seen with their own eyes. In 1967, David Roberts and his Harvard Mountaineering Club cohorts ventured to an unnamed group of mountains at the southern rampart of the Alaska Range. Art Davidson's toes still tingled with frostbite from his winter on Denali, but he rounded out the crew. Fifty-two days in the Range left them with a slew of first ascents, but their primary objectives, including a peak they called the Angel, were left unclimbed. As the first climbers to enter the Range, they christened them the Revelation Mountains. Roberts would become a successful author of more than twenty books, many of them about his experiences in Alaska. In his 2006 memoir *On the Ridge Between Life*

and Death, Roberts devoted nearly an entire chapter to his Revelation expedition.

As I searched for my own unique path, his words lit a fire within me: "No peak within forty miles of North Buttress in any direction had ever been climbed, or, as far as I could tell, even attempted." He crowed, "Here, I thought greedily, lay one of the last challenges of its kind in North America—difficult first ascents of unclimbed peaks in an unnamed range, weeks of prowling across terrain that no humans had ever explored." Little had changed when I first ventured to the Revelations in 2008, forty-one years later. At the time, few photographs of the peaks existed online or in historical climbing books. Fueled by Roberts's statement, I began to pluck off as many of the remaining first ascents as possible before other climbers took notice. My shining goal, and the central focus of my life at the time, was to complete the first ascent of Mount Mausolus (9170 feet, or 2795 meters), a remote peak that Roberts had called "a hopeless labyrinth" and "perhaps the toughest climb in the range" in the 1968 issue of the *American Alpine Journal.* Armed with a single grainy photograph from a local pilot, Seth Holden and I spent three expeditions trying to climb its 4500-foot ice-coated west face.

As our technical skills increased on first ascents of lesser nearby peaks, Mausolus remained as malignant and ghostly as its arching shadows. On our third year, we landed directly under the west face. The mountain exuded a miasmatic force of negative energy. During the coldest part of the night we raced up the lower shroud of the face, but a feeling of death hung in the air. Avalanches roared down our route within hours of returning to camp. We flew to another part of the

Range and were soon staring up at Roberts's Angel. Under perfect skies and with three days of supplies, we attempted the South Ridge, the route Roberts and his team had tried five times. On their last attempt they stopped just seven hundred feet short of the summit. Seth and I retreated well below Roberts's high point. He and I would never share a rope again.

Several months later Seth died in a plane crash not far from the Revelations. His death left a void but also inspired me to fulfill our dream. The next year, I finally stood atop Mount Mausolus, having completed the most difficult climb of my life. I released Seth's ashes to the summit winds in a final act of friendship.

Four years of cavorting around the Revelations had filled my mind with an endless list of new climbs, but Carl Battreall's photographs of the Angel gave me pause. Our previous jaunt up the South Ridge had left me questioning how we would descend thirty-five hundred feet of unknown terrain. Not even I had seen the other sides of the mountain, but Carl's photo profiled a perfect couloir snaking all the way to the valley floor. It would make an ideal descent route should we ever reach the summit. In 2012 my partner, Ben Trocki, and I completed Roberts's vision of the South Ridge in twenty-one hours round-trip. It was comforting to know beforehand that the descent would be a casual affair instead of thirty-five hundred feet of rappelling through unknown terrain.

CERTAIN MOUNTAINS AND ROUTES TAKE on legendary statures. Sometimes it's the natural architecture: a scourge of ice illuminated between protruding buttresses. Other times it's the history of a line; a zealous team returning again and again to finish a coveted dream.

The North Buttress of Mount Hunter (at 6100 feet, or 1829 meters) is one of those unique features—visually awe inspiring, extremely difficult, and full of illustrious history. Towering brazenly above Denali base camp, it remains one of the ultimate test-pieces for technical climbers. Starting in the mid-1970s, a number of the world's foremost alpinists turned their attention to the North Buttress. In 1980, Washington climbers Doug Klewin, Rob Newsom, and Pat and Dan McNerthney made significant progress. Poor weather forced them off after forging nearly a dozen pitches. For several years they had attempted other potential routes on the North Buttress, even making it near the top of the

North Buttress Couloir before breaking their picks in the bullet-hard ice.

They returned in 1981. While they were climbing above a feature called the Prow, Mugs Stump, perhaps America's most accomplished alpinist at the time, flew in with New Zealander Paul Aubrey and pushed a line slightly right of their original start. The Washington team descended to repair a broken portaledge, while Stump and Aubrey surpassed them and continued upward through virgin terrain. Newsom exclaimed at base camp that watching them climb high on the buttress was "like having your girlfriend stolen from you." Several days later, Mugs and Aubrey climbed through

the end of the major technical difficulties at twelve thousand feet. Although more than twenty-five hundred feet separated them from the summit of Mount Hunter, they claimed a first ascent and rappelled to base camp.

In 1983, Klewin returned with Todd Bibler. In the finest of styles, they climbed their original line on the North Buttress of Mount Hunter to the summit and finalized their vision. To crown the early history of the North Buttress, Newsom and Pat McNerthney returned and climbed the route to the summit for its second complete ascent in 1984. McNerthney brilliantly free-climbed the Shaft, a four-hundred-foot chimney of dead vertical and overhanging ice that is the route's crux.

I'M OLDER NOW. MY CHEEKS have grown more resilient against the wind, my senses more attuned to the changing movement of clouds. After nearly twenty expeditions into different parts of this broad arch of mountains called the Alaska Range, I am still plagued by an insatiable hunger of discovery and challenge. Distant corners of this chaotic landscape feel familiar. My mind overlays the mountains with stories both experienced and imagined. Mount Hunter once seemed unattainable, but years of focus have slowly expanded my sense of possibility.

Halfway up the towering North Buttress, shards of gray ice splinter as I swing my tool, echoing a high-pitched *tink, tink, tink* as they ricochet out of sight. The tips of my crampons bite precariously into the vertical wall of polished ice and my calves scream for relief. Deep breathing helps to calm my fried nerves as I stare up an endless flow encased between looming granite walls. The frayed rope hangs away from the wall to a distant ice screw. We have been awake for more than twenty-four hours and real sleep is still several days away. There isn't even a spot big enough to sit for another five hundred feet. As a young man, this is what I envisioned when climbing huge, difficult routes in Alaska: wavering between the spectrum of doubt and self-belief, fear and momentary courage.

Twenty-four hours of sleepless climbing later, every plunge step through knee-deep snow toward Mount Hunter's summit is a journey in itself. The few ingested calories tease my writhing stomach. We stop to melt water with the remnants of our stove gas. Without sleeping bags, we huddle together until relentless cold wills us to continue moving. I squint as wind lashes my face. Our footsteps fall off the North Buttress. Sixty hours of near constant movement clouds my alertness, but a magnetized focus pulls me upward. As we stagger onto the summit of Mount Hunter, a decade of dreaming culminates into this singular clarifying moment. I wrap my arms around my partners. We laugh between dry coughs, and happy tears freeze around my eyes. A momentary feeling of transcendence overcomes me. I ponder the chronology as it evolved from impossible to an achievable goal and now: a building block to even greater challenges.

I believe each person is gifted with only a few opportunities to choose the compass bearing of his or her life. My revelation came when I realized that somewhere upon those distant icy peaks was the path to my self-discovery. Through these experiences I have found the courage to follow my heart. Those split-second decisions that divide life from death have honed my instincts in other parts of life. I have formed bonds that eclipse friendship and trust that defies explanation. Summit vistas and moments of laughter echoing off remote walls are forever imprinted upon my mind. During moments of raw survival the facade of my hubris has been stripped away to reveal my brightest and darkest self.

Climbing in Alaska has given me perspective, challenges, goals, and dreams. Mountains are my venue for staring fear in the face and screaming at it. I take prudence not to underestimate a mountain or overestimate myself, but to avoid risk is the most dangerous path I could take. Without this perspective, I would not truly know myself. Without challenges, dreams cannot thrive. Dreams burgeon an unrelenting imagination.

As I grow, my mind expands to new possibilities and slowly cuts away the impossible. My imagination runs wild, because it has been proven time and time again that the limits of possibility are constrained solely by the limitations of our imagination.

Babel Tower and South Buttress reflected in a tarn, Revelation Mountains

Talkeetna Air Taxi's Paul Roderick drops Sy Cloud and me off on the Tatina Glacier, Kichatna Mountains, Denali National Park and Preserve.

PHOTOGRAPHING THE ALASKA RANGE
FLYING LOW AND SLOW
CARL BATTREALL

My stomach was twisted in knots, a combination of hunger and anxiety. We had begun to ration our food, not knowing if we would be escaping our mountain prison anytime soon. We were in the Kichatna Mountains, a landscape of unrivaled rugged beauty. Monolith after monolith surged out of the glaciers, creating an area that has the largest concentration of granite spires in Alaska. I had always wanted to visit the rock empire of the Kichatnas, where only the boldest alpinists ventured. What had deterred me for years from finalizing an expedition was the area's reputation for some of the worst weather in the Alaska Range. At the far west corner of Denali National Park and Preserve, the Kichatnas are the prow of the central Alaska Range ship. Storms from the south and the west hit these mountains with full force. Rumor has it that the Kichatnas get four nice days of weather for every thirty terrible days. Needless to say, they are not visitor friendly.

On our fourth day, like clockwork, the wind picked up. We had had glorious weather up to that point, so we knew our luck would run out. We dragged our sleds up the Cul-de-Sac Glacier, heading toward the base of the Kichatna Spire. With each mile the wind grew stronger, forcing us to forgo the stellar views, heads bent down instead, watching our skis slide back and forth in a mind-numbing rhythm. Pressing our advance into the ever increasing wind was pointless. We needed to dig in and make camp.

My partner, Sy, went to work crafting snow blocks of the highest quality, a skill he had mastered after countless glacier trips. I dug deeper into the glacier. We had only planned to stay on the Cul-de-Sac Glacier for a day or two, then move on to the Shadows Glacier for pickup. But the Kichatnas had made other plans for us. On our fifth day of waiting, a day after our scheduled pickup, I began to wonder if our plane would be able to make it to us. We had long passed the option of skiing out of the mountains; our fate was completely in the hands of the pilot.

WHEN I FIRST BEGAN PHOTOGRAPHING the Alaska Range, I was thirty years old, full of energy and stubbornness. I wanted to reach as many locations without using planes or motorized vehicles. It was a flawed plan. There are few access points into the extremely isolated Alaska Range. The Kichatna Mountains, for example, are more than a hundred miles from any major road. Loaded with camera gear and other equipment, I would require weeks to cross endless bogs and unforgiving rivers, just to reach the base of the mountains. My team could use light and fast tactics, covering ground much quicker, but this wouldn't allow for meaningful photography and exploring: the two main reasons I work in the mountains. Airplanes were going to play a vital role in the success of the project.

Since then, I have flown in all types of bush planes: Super Cubs, 180s, Beavers, and Otters. I have landed on floats, skis, and cartoon-size "tundra tires." I have had some exciting landings and have seen some amazing sights. Alaskan bush flying traces its roots back to the Alaska Range, particularly to the Thoroughfare River and the pilot Carl Ben Eielson. Eielson made some of the first off-runway landings, in his open cockpit biplane.

On one historic landing in the early 1920s, on the wide braided-river bar below the now aptly named Eielson Visitor Center in Denali National Park, Eielson landed a miner and his gear, cutting the miner's approach time by weeks. The bush plane's potential to "open up" remote Alaska thus became a reality. Eielson became an international hero, the first to fly across both the Arctic and Antarctic. Eielson died in 1929 at the early age of thirty-two, in a plane crash while trying to rescue some sailors who were stranded in the sea ice off of Cape North in Siberia.

Over time, pilots increased the size of their tires, allowing for even more difficult and rough landings. Floats were added to smaller and smaller planes and, ultimately, skis were used, allowing mountaineers to reach the big mountains without the epic approaches. More important than the planes are those who fly them. Alaskan bush pilots are a special breed, especially the mountain flyers. Many Alaskan pilots never venture into the big mountains. There is a fear, mostly unwarranted, about flying in and around these enormous ranges. But there have been very few crashes there. Most bush plane crashes happen on air strip landings and takeoffs or when flying in poor weather—something mountain pilots rarely do.

Many of Alaska's bush pilots are seasonal, coming up for the summer to fly tourists around. Most flight services don't offer exploratory flying (flying and landing in new terrain, away from the established spots). If they do offer it, there are only one or two pilots experienced enough and it will likely cost a fortune. Unfortunately, experienced mountain and glacier pilots are becoming rare. Many of the pilots I have flown with over the decades are in their sixties and nearing retirement. They learned to fly with their fathers and grew up wanting to be bush pilots. Many of the pilots I know, who are the only ones flying into certain sections of the Alaska Range, don't have children itching to follow their lead. When they retire, a specialized knowledge of the mountains, glaciers, rivers, and wildlife will be lost. Access to many secluded mountain areas will vanish. Thanks to these talented pilots, I love the excitement of flying and doing aerial photography, although it can sometimes be a little scary. It's fun flying in slow planes, a few hundred feet above mountain ridges and splintered glaciers.

ONE CRISP OCTOBER EVENING IN 2013, I was on a flight with my friend Dan, a fellow photographer who owns a little Cessna 120. We decided to head over Merrill Pass, which splits the Neacola Mountains from the Tordrillo and Hidden mountains. Dan's bare-bones Cessna is the perfect photo plane. It flies low and slow and the windows open up nice and wide. There are no fancy gizmos onboard his plane; in fact, on this flight the cockpit's electrical system wasn't even working, which meant no lights inside. The low evening light was beautiful. When we reached Merrill Pass, a wall of fog stopped us. We aborted our original plan and circled around. To the south we could see a collection of spectacular peaks, bathed in glorious light, so we headed straight for them. They were the high peaks of the Neacolas, Mount Neacola being the tallest at 9426 feet (2873 meters). One particular peak, the Citadel, demanded our attention, with its seductive ridges and smooth granite faces plastered in ice.

Pilot and photographer, Dan doesn't miss a shot. When photographing a peak, we often circle it so both of us can get images. I remember one moment, I was shooting out my open window, the cold wind trying to suck the life out of my fingers, when I looked in front of us: the window was filled with a granite wall. Dan was calmly photographing out his own wide-open window. "Uh, Dan, there is a huge mountain in front of us!" I called. Looking ahead, Dan shut his window, pulled the throttle, and coolly maneuvered us away from the icy spire.

We flew around those peaks for an hour. The light wouldn't quit; it kept getting nicer, from yellow to pink to red to magenta. When the final color vanished from the peaks, it was almost dark and we were in the middle of the mountains, more than a hundred miles from Anchorage. We rushed down one of the glaciers to its outflow and followed the last light reflected off the river. Dan and I made it out into the open country as the last glimmer of light vanished from the horizon. There weren't any large mountains between us and Anchorage, whose lights glowed far off in the distance. Flying in darkness, we used headlamps to keep a watchful eye on our diminishing fuel.

The roar of the engine kept us awake. While that memorable trip may have been a little too risky for my blood, the photographs I took during that flight are some of the best I have ever taken.

THE MIND CAN PLAY TRICKS on you when you're waiting for a plane out in the vast white wilderness. You keep thinking that you hear something. Out in the Kichatnas with Sy, a few days beyond our scheduled pickup, our brief optimal weather window was again vanishing. The clouds were descending, the wind gusts increasing. The mountains were closing their grip. We had called our flight service numerous times, letting them know that it looked good, but when they got in the air, all they could see was a wall of black clouds in our direction. Defeated, I began to unpack my gear. I dreaded the decision on what food I was going to ration. My stomach growled. Then I heard it.

"Sy!" I yelled. "The plane!" He was skiing up and down the runway, packing it down. Silence returned. The wind whipped snow up in swirls. Had I fooled myself again? "It must be the wind." And then a lion's roar came raging through the Spires. The sound was deafening as it echoed around the granite amphitheater. My heart racing, I hastily took down the tent. The great mechanical bird would save us again.

LEFT Thunder Peak, Denali National Park and Preserve

RIGHT Weathered rocks, looking toward the Lime Hills from the Revelation Mountains

Sandwiched between the Revelation and Tordrillo mountains is a sea of nameless, unclimbed peaks known as the Hidden Mountains.

ACKNOWLEDGMENTS

Sy Cloud skiing by an ice cave on the lower Ruth Glacier, Denali National Park and Preserve

FIRST AND FOREMOST, I MUST thank my parents, Dan and Sharon Battreall, who have always encouraged me and supported my countless wild schemes for grand adventure and my numerous artistic undertakings. I must also thank my high school photography teacher, Doyel Riley, who believed in my work and persuaded me to make photography my career.

A project of this scale could never be completed alone. In fact, I have never considered this project a solo endeavor; instead, it has been a collaboration between those who love Alaska's mountains and the Alaska Range.

I have made many solo trips into the mountains, but the trips that have a lasting impression are those made with friends. Sy Cloud and Opie Combs have gone on more expeditions with me than I can remember. It is not easy traveling with a photographer, and few adventurers are willing to sacrifice their own goals for the sake of photography. Sy and Opie selflessly endured more suffering for this project than any of my other companions, and without their good humor and resilience in the mountains under extreme conditions, this book would not exist.

I have had heaps of support from family and friends including: Amy and Shane Fitch, Barry and Joyce Weiss, Florian Schulz and Emil Herrera-Schulz, Salomon Schulz, Javid Kamali, Stacey Cooper, Jeff and Jess Rigby, Phil Barnes and Laura Harris, Nathaniel Wilder, Chris and Mara Wrobel, Peter Lloyd and Karen West, Dave Dempsey, Dan Bailey, Kevin "OE" Robbins, Dan Oberlatz, Mike Morganson, and Jon Cornforth.

I received a lot of support from a variety of great companies and organizations including: The Alaska Conservation Foundation, Adventurers and Scientists for Conservation, Denali Cabins, Project Pressure, Alaska Alpine Adventures, K2 Aviation, Patagonia, Black Diamond, and the Anchorage REI.

The climbing community has stood behind this project since its conception. Many organizations, publications, and individuals have gone above and beyond to share this project with the world including: The Mountaineering Club of Alaska, the American Alpine Club, *Alpinist* magazine, Planet Mountain, *Adventure Journal*, Matt Samet, Matt Helliker, Steve Gruhn, and the late Ryan Jennings.

Photography books are expensive to publish. Thanks to those Kickstarter supporters who contributed extra to make this book possible: Neil Murphy, Larry Ashbacher, Dustin Engelken, Brian Garcia, Steve Ingle, John Hess, Galen Flint, Carole Sheehan, Laura Custard Hurt, David Allan Smith, Matt Linehan, James Ghoslin, Maxine Vehlow, David and Kay Wood, Steven Miley, Kenneth Harely, Amy Reams, Roland Kilcher, Amy Finkelstein, Myles Steiner, Chris Jungman, Benjamin Erdmann, Wayne Pence, Carl Johnson, Dana Williams, Ronette Snyder, Sarah Tingey, Jim Dewitt, Sam Kikuchi, Sumit Bhardwaj, Jerrold Mathews, and Bill Romberg.

Special thanks to Kate Rogers, who had faith in this project and worked hard to make sure it became a reality. Thanks to Laura Shauger, Jen Grable, Ani Rucki, and all the rest of the wonderful crew at Mountaineers Books, who put in many long hours creating a beautiful book that will be treasured for years to come.

And thanks to the contributing writers: Art Davidson, Roman Dial, Verna Pratt, Bill Sherwonit, Brian Okonek, Jeff Benowitz, and Clint Helander. Your voices elevated this book from a simple photography tribute to a grand celebration of the mighty Alaska Range!

And finally my wife, Pam, and son, Walker, my favorite companions in life and adventure, who have sacrificed more than anyone to make this book happen, I love you both.

INDEX

A

Adkins, Paul, 28, 36, 39
Alaska Range, 27-28
    historical summits, 113-133
    map, 12
    modern climbing in, 139-159
    orogenesis of, 45-62
    reflections on flora, 69-78
    wildlife residents, 85-107
Angel, The, Revelation Mountains, 150, 151
Arctic ground squirrel, 101
Arctic tern, 97, 101
Aubrey, Paul, 152-153

B

Babel Tower, Revelation Mountains, 155
Backside Glacier, Denali NP, 65
Barrill, Edward, 126
Battreall, Carl, 22, 151
bears
    black, 106-107
    grizzly, 86, 89, 94, 96-97, 100-102, 105-106
Beckey, Fred, 121, 145
Benowitz, Jeff Apple, 22, 45
Bering Land Bridge, 20
Bernd, Ed, 147
Bibler, Todd, 153
birds, 97-98
Black Crap, 49
Black Rapids Glacier, Hayes Range, 14-15, 64, 130
bog plants, 70
Bristol Bay, 62
Broken Tooth, Denali NP, 123
Brooks, Alfred, 48-49, 117, 128
Brooks Range, 53
Browne, Belmore, 126
Browne Tower, 128
bush pilots, 158

C

Capps Glacier, Tordrillo Mountains, 145
caribou, 84-85, 92, 104-105, 110
Cassin, Ricardo, 122
Chakachamina Lake, 108-109, 135
Chelatna Lake, Denali NP, 146
Chulitna River, 99
Citadel, The, 13, 21, 158
Clearwater Mountains, 124

climbing in the Alaska Range, 139-159
Cloud, Sy, 41, 59, 60, 104, 114, 132, 143, 156, 159, 164
club moss, 31
collared pikas, 89-90
Combs, Opie, 114, 159
Cook, Dr. Frederick, 126
Cook Inlet, 113
Cul-de-Sac Glacier, Kichatna Mountains, 157

D

Dall, William Healey, 114
Dall sheep, 31, 32, 86, 90, 92, 93-94
Davidson, Art, 15, 120, 147, 148
Delta Mountains, 18, 31, 35, 105, 110-111, 127, 149
Delta River, 116
Denali, 15, 27, 48, 54, 57, 82-83, 87, 98, 99, 113-114, 118, 121, 128, 132, 136
Denali Diamond, 148
Denali Fault, 32, 46, 48, 51, 52, 53, 54, 57
Denali Massif, 35, 117
Denali National Park and Preserve, 19, 28, 35, 51, 61, 102, 114
Denali Pass, 16, 125
Denali State Park, 159
Dial, Roman, 22, 27
Dickey, William, 114

E

Eielson, Carl Ben, 157
Eielson Visitor Center, Denali NP, 157
Eldridge, George, 117
Eldridge Glacier, Denali NP, 28
Entropy Wall, Hayes Range, 148

F

Flat Top Spire, Kichatna Mountains, 152
flora of Alaska Range, 69-78

G

Gabriel Icefall, Gulkana Glacier, Delta Mountains, 126
Gakona Glacier, 58
Gakona Glacier, Delta Mountains, 62-63
Genet, Ray, 120, 147
Gerstle Glacier, Delta Mountains, 16
Gillam Glacier, Hayes Range, 52
glacial rivers, 130-133

Great Gorge of Ruth Glacier, 36
Great Icefall, Muldrow Glacier, 129
grizzly bears, 86, 89, 94, 96-97, 100-102, 105-106

H

Hale, Matt, 147
Haley, Colin, 148
Harper, Walter, 118
Harper Glacier, 125, 128
Harrer, Heinrich, 121, 145
Harvard Route, Denali, 147-148
harvesting wild plants, 78
Healy, 35
Healy Creek, 97, 170
Helander, Clint, 22, 139
Herron, Lieutenant, 120, 128
Hess Mountain, 35
Hidden Mountains, Lake Clark NP, 27, 34, 58-59, 158, 162
historical summits of Alaska Range, 113-133
Holden, Seth, 142, 151
House, Steve, 148

I

Iditarod Trail, 128
Igitna Peak, Hidden Mountains, 27

J

Jensen, Don, 147
Johnston, Dave, 120, 147
Jumbo Dome, Healy, 53

K

Kahiltna Glacier, 118, 122, 132, 149
Kantishna, 117
Karstens, Harry, 118, 128, 129
Kenibuna Lake, Neacola Mountains, 34, 101, 147
Kennedy, Michael, 118
Kichatna Mountains, 36, 46, 53, 54, 157, 159
Kichatna Spires, 15, 127, 156, 157, 159
Kijik River, 39
Klewin, Doug, 152, 153

L

Lake Clark, 28, 39
Lake Clark National Park and Preserve, 19, 21
lithosphere of the earth, 48
Lowe, George, 118

M

map of Alaska Range, 12
McKinley, William, 114
McNerthney, Pat and Dan, 152, 153
Mentasta Mountains, 31
Merrill Pass, 27, 158
Meybohm, Henry, 121, 145
Middle Triple Peak, Kichatna Mountains, 141
Moffit, Fred, 48–49
monkshood, 88
Monolith Pass, Kichatna Mountains, 143
Moore Icefall, Delta Mountains, 17, 96
moose, 81, 88, 95, 98
Mooses Tooth, Denali NP, 123, 127, 142
Mount Balchen, Hayes Range, 53, 56
Mount Barrille, Denali NP, 134
Mount Brooks, 51
Mount Church, Denali NP, 29
Mount Crosson, 122
Mount Dall, Denali NP, 112–113
Mount Deborah, Denali NP, 35, 53, 114, 121, 125, 145
Mount Dickey, 127
Mount Foraker, Denali NP, 25, 36, 48, 53, 57, 114, 118, 120, 122, 127, 132
Mount Frances, 122
Mount Geist, Hayes Range, 56
Mount Hayes, 40, 53, 71, 125
Mount Hesperus, Revelation Mountains, 66
Mount Hess, Hayes Ridge, 125, 129
Mount Hunter, Denali NP, 36, 121, 122, 132, 146, 148, 149, 151–154
Mount Huntington, 127, 141, 147, 148
Mount Johnson, Ruth Gorge, Denali NP, 42–43
Mount Kimball, 31
Mount Mausolus, Revelation Mountains, 151
Mount McKinley (Denali), 27, 48, 90, 114. See Denali
Mount Moffit, Eastern Alaska Range, 20, 51
Mount Neacola, 158
Mount Neana, 57
Mount Shand, Hayes Range, 37
Mount Spurr, Tordrillo Mountains, 108
Muldrow, Robert, 117
Muldrow Glacier, 118, 129
Murie, Adolph, 90, 92
Murphy, Neil, 149

N

Nabesna River, 31
Nanga Parbat, 145
Neacola Mountains, 21, 34, 107, 130–131, 140, 158
Nelson, Brad, 149
Nenana River, Denali NP, 39

Newsom, Rob, 152, 153
Nutzotin Mountains, Wrangell–St. Elias NP, 28, 30, 46, 57, 59–60, 66

O

Okonek, Brian, 22, 113
On the Ridge Between Life and Death (Roberts), 148, 151

P

Parker, Herschel, 126
Peak 8505, 13
Pebble Mine, Bristol Bay, 62
petite anadyr draba, 73
pikas, collared, 89–90
Plains of Murie, 102
plants of Alaska Range, 69–78
Polychrome Glacier, Denali NP, 103
Polychrome Hills, Denali NP, 55
Pratt, Verna, 22, 69

R

Revelation Mountains, 36, 49, 148
Roberts, David, 127, 147, 148, 151
Roderick, Paul, 156
Rosen, Yereth, 133
rosewort, 61
Rowell, Galen, 127
Ruth Amphitheater, Denali NP, 41
Ruth Glacier, Denali NP, 119, 126, 140, 144, 145, 146, 164
Ruth Gorge, 57, 134, 142

S

Sable Pass, 85, 86
Sanctuary River, 20
sandhill cranes, 97–98
sastrugi formations, 111, 128
sawyer beetle, 51
semipalmated plover, 116
Shaft, the, Denali NP, 153
Shamrock Glacier, Neacola Mountains, 24, 92, 106
Shamrock Lake, Neacola Mountains, 108–109
Sheldon, Charles, 17, 19, 90
Sherwonit, Bill, 22, 85
South Buttress, Revelation Mountains, 155
Stony River, 36, 39
Stuck, Hudson, 118, 128, 129
Stump, Mugs, 152–153
summits of Alaska Range, 113–133
Susitna Glacier, 44–45, 57
Susitna River, 113, 114

T

Tackle, Jack, 148
Tangle Lake, Amphitheater Mountains, 75
Tatina Glacier, Kichatna Mountains, 122, 156
Tatina River, 36
Tatum, Robert, 118
Teklanika River, 20, 38
Telaquana Trail, 39
Teocalli Mountains, 30, 36
Terra Cotta Mountains, 36
Terray, Lionel, 127, 146
Thayer, Elton, 126
Thunder Peak, Denali NP, 160
Tobin, Carl, 28, 36
Tordrillo Mountains, 53, 58, 108–109, 122, 135, 158
tree line alpine zone, 73
Trident Glacier, Hayes Range, 80
Triumvirate Glacier, Tordrillo Mountains, 122
Trocki, Ben, 151
Twight, Mark, 148

U

USGS research hut, Gulkana Glacier, 40
Usibelli Coal Mine, 35

V

Van Ballenberghe, Vic, 98, 101
Vancouver, Captain George, 113–114

W

Ward, Ed, 127
Washburn, Dr. Bradford, 118, 125, 146, 148
Waterfall Creek, Clearwater Mountains, 82
Waterman, John, 140, 148
West Kahiltna Peak, 122
Westman, Mark, 148
Wickersham Wall, Denali, 35
wilderness designation, 19–20
wildlife residents of Alaska Range, 85–107
wolves, 19, 20, 86, 89, 102
Wonder Lake, 17, 128
woolly lousewort, 19
wormwood, 76, 78
Wrangell Mountains, 59
Wrangellia, 51
Wrangell–St. Elias National Park and Preserve, 19, 31
Wrobel, Chris, 114

Y

Yentna Glacier, Denali NP, 78
Yentna River, 91
Yukon River, 114

ABOUT THE PHOTOGRAPHER & THE CONTRIBUTORS

Nathaniel Wilder

Carl Battreall has been working as a photographer for more than two decades. Since moving to Alaska in 2001, Carl has focused on photographing Alaska's most remote and isolated alpine regions. He has explored more than two hundred glaciers in fourteen different mountain ranges in Alaska and the Nepal Himalaya. Carl is a Rasmuson Foundation artist fellow and the recipient of the Alaska Conservation Foundation's Daniel Housberg Wilderness Image Award. His photographs and articles appear regularly in books, magazines, and calendars throughout the world. His first book, *Chugach State Park: Alaska's Backyard Wilderness*, was published by Greatland Graphics in 2011. Carl lives in Anchorage with his wife, Pam, and son, Walker.

Jeff Apple Benowitz has spent the past twenty-six years climbing the famously obscure across the breadth of the Alaska Range from the Thorn (eastern), Southeast Spur of Hunter (central) and North Ridge of Kichatna Spire (western Alaska Range). The time he has spent debating with the wind has inspired him to use climbing stories as metaphors for life, including writing many an essay for *Alpinist*, *Climbing*, and *Rock and Ice*. As a PhD geochronologist at the University of Alaska Geophysical Institute, Jeff has devoted his research to getting at the backstory of his mountain home. He also learned along the way that if you tell your spouse you are going to the mountains for work, she won't notice your wedding ring is inscribed with the Alaska Range skyline.

Art Davidson grew up in Colorado, where he spent summers fishing and climbing in the Rockies. At 21, he hitchhiked to Alaska, and began climbing in the Chugach, Wrangles, Kichatnas, and Revelations, as well as the Alaska Range. He raised his children in a home he built in the mountains near Anchorage. He has spearheaded many cultural and environmental initiatives, including the creation of Chugach State Park. Davidson has authored a number of books, including *Minus 148°*, about the first winter ascent of Denali, and *Endangered Peoples*, about the challenges facing indigenous people around the world.

By skate, ski, pedal, paddle, and foot, **Roman Dial** has crossed 14,000 miles of roadless Alaska, making first ascents of rock spires, frozen waterfalls, and alpine faces, as well as first descents of rivers and canyons. In 1986 he traversed 1000 miles across the Brooks Range. In 1996 he traversed the Alaska Range, and in 2006 he walked 625 miles across America's largest wilderness, the most remote region of the Brooks Range, without resupply. He has published photos and stories in *National Geographic, Smithsonian, Outside*, and the *Patagonia* catalog, as well as *Alaska, Bicycling, Rock and Ice, Backpacker*, and *Cross-Country Skier*. He is the author of *Packrafting!* Living in Anchorage with his wife, Peggy, Roman teaches ecology, statistics, and outdoor studies at Alaska Pacific University.

Clint Helander is recognized as one of Alaska's leading young alpinists and has made a name for himself by climbing bold, hard routes and accomplishing visionary first ascents. Clint

was born and raised in Washington State, but moved to Alaska in 2003 for college. It was there that he began climbing and fell in love with the big mountains of Alaska. In this inhospitable and ever-changing landscape, he experiences the purest elements of life and companionship. After nearly twenty expeditions into various parts of the Alaska Range, the pull is as strong as ever. This avid freelance writer's stories and articles have appeared in a multitude of climbing-oriented publications, including *Alpinist* and the *American Alpine Journal*.

Brian Okonek is a legendary mountaineer and son of the famed bush pilot Jim Okonek. Brian and his wife, Diane, owned and directed Alaska-Denali Guiding Inc., specializing in guided expeditions up Denali and the surrounding peaks from 1984 to 2000. He has climbed many peaks in the Denali region and travelled extensively through the rugged country that surrounds the mountain. With each trip, his appreciation for what the early explorers of the area accomplished has grown. Nearly everywhere he has gone, he has crossed the paths of those who made the first attempts and climbs of Denali. His photographs of climbing in the Range have been published in many books and magazines. He has written articles for climbing publications and contributed to several books about climbing Denali.

Verna Pratt grew up in a rural area in Massachusetts and moved to Alaska

in 1966. She quickly fell in love with alpine plants. Studying, photographing, and growing alpines became her main focus. Verna founded the Alaska Native Plant Society in 1982 and the Alaska Rock Garden Society in 1997. This opened up the world of leading field trips and lecturing on native plants throughout Alaska, nationally, and internationally. Verna is the author of five books on native plants, including *Wildflowers of Denali National Park*. She helps maintain native plantings at the Campbell Creek Science Center and the alpine rock gardens at the Alaska Botanical Garden, while teaching outdoor classes in Denali Park through the Murie Science Center and in the Chugach Mountains through Alaska Geographic.

Born in Bridgeport, Connecticut, nature writer **Bill Sherwonit** has called Alaska home since 1982. He has contributed essays to a wide variety of newspapers, magazines, journals, and anthologies and is the author of more than a dozen books. His most recent books include *Animal Stories: Encounters with Alaska's Wildlife, Changing Paths: Travels and Meditations in Alaska's Arctic Wilderness*, and *Living with Wildness: An Alaskan Odyssey*. Sherwonit's work focuses on Alaska's wildlife and wildlands, but he's passionate about wild nature in all its varied forms, including the nature of his adopted hometown, Anchorage, and the spirited wildness we carry within us.

Bands of coal, near Healy Creek

MOUNTAINEERS BOOKS is a leading publisher of mountaineering literature and guides—including our flagship title, *Mountaineering: The Freedom of the Hills*—as well as adventure narratives, natural history, and general outdoor recreation. Through our two imprints, Skipstone and Braided River, we also publish titles on sustainability and conservation. We are committed to supporting the environmental and educational goals of our organization by providing expert information on human-powered adventure, sustainable practices at home and on the trail, and preservation of wilderness.

The Mountaineers, founded in 1906, is a 501(c)(3) nonprofit outdoor activity and conservation organization whose mission is "to explore, study, preserve, and enjoy the natural beauty of the outdoors." One of the largest such organizations in the United States, it sponsors classes and year-round outdoor activities throughout the Pacific Northwest, including climbing, hiking, backcountry skiing, snowshoeing, bicycling, camping, paddling, and more. The Mountaineers also supports its mission through its publishing division, Mountaineers Books, and promotes environmental education and citizen engagement.

Our publications are made possible through the generosity of donors and through sales of more than 600 titles on outdoor recreation, sustainable lifestyle, and conservation. To donate, purchase books, or learn more, visit us online.

MOUNTAINEERS BOOKS
1001 SW Klickitat Way, Suite 201 • Seattle, WA 98134
800-553-4453 • mbooks@mountaineersbooks.org • www.mountaineersbooks.org

OTHER TITLES FROM MOUNTAINEERS BOOKS

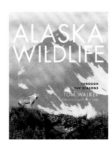

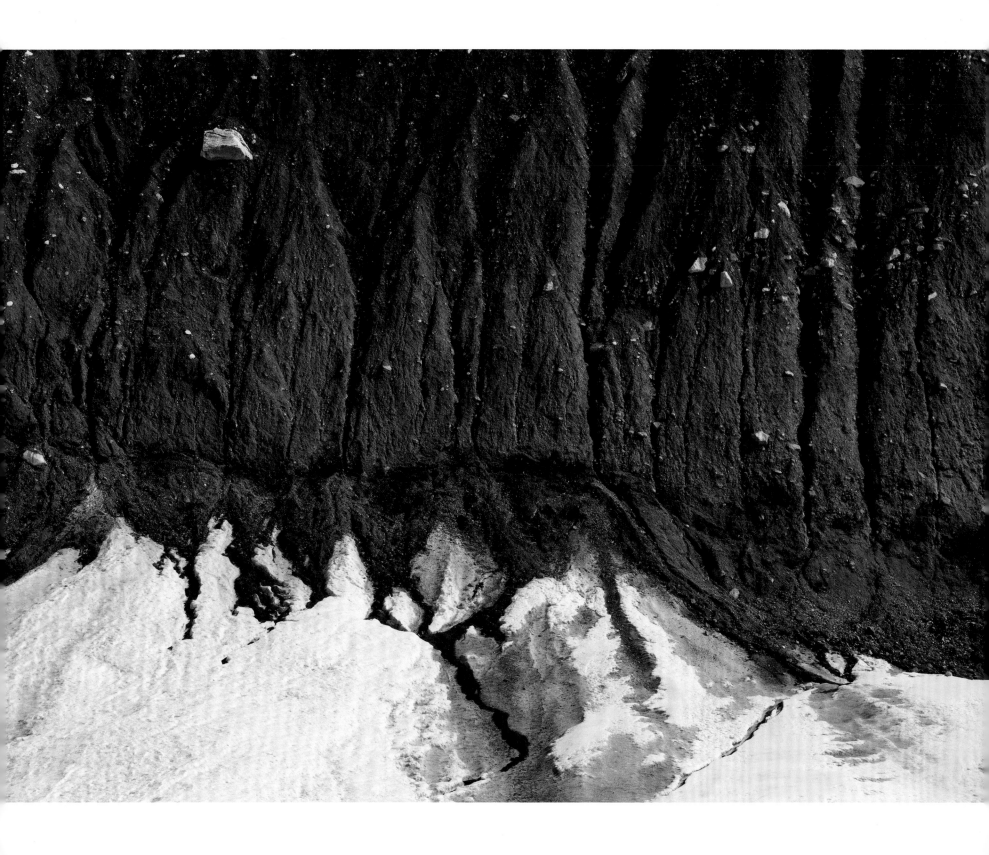